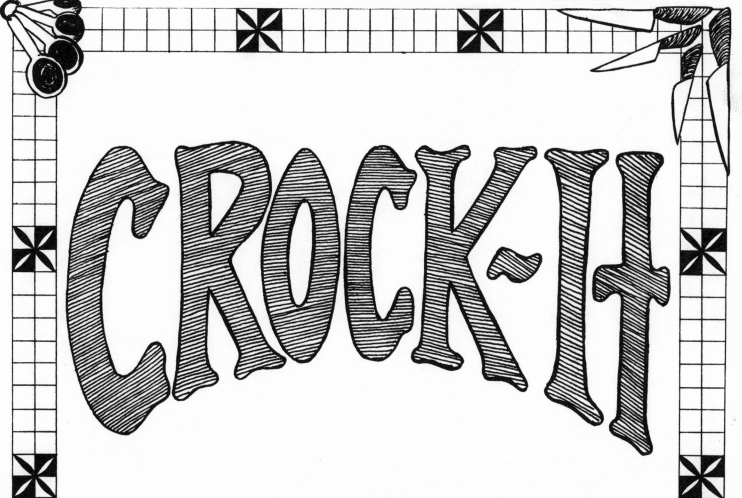

CROCK-IT

Created, Collected, and Converted
by Barbara M. Neslen, R.N.

Illustrated
by Allene Ramsey

Consultant
Allison A. Jones, M.S.R.D.

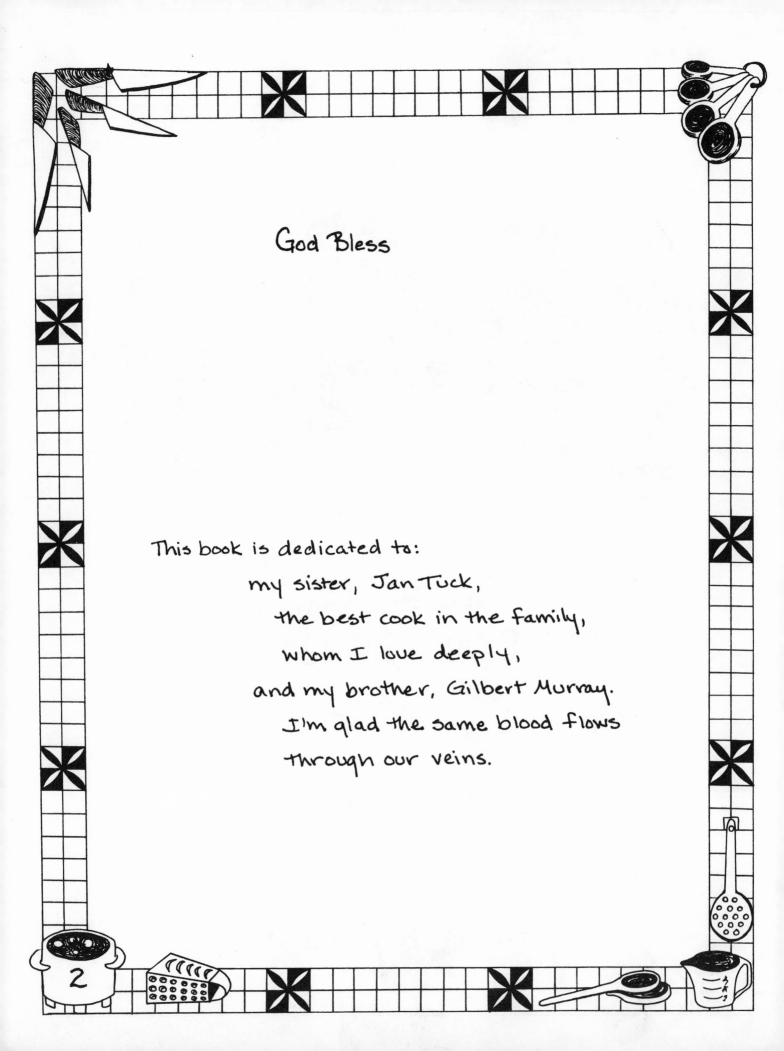

God Bless

This book is dedicated to:
     my sister, Jan Tuck,
       the best cook in the family,
       whom I love deeply,
    and my brother, Gilbert Murray.
       I'm glad the same blood flows
       through our veins.

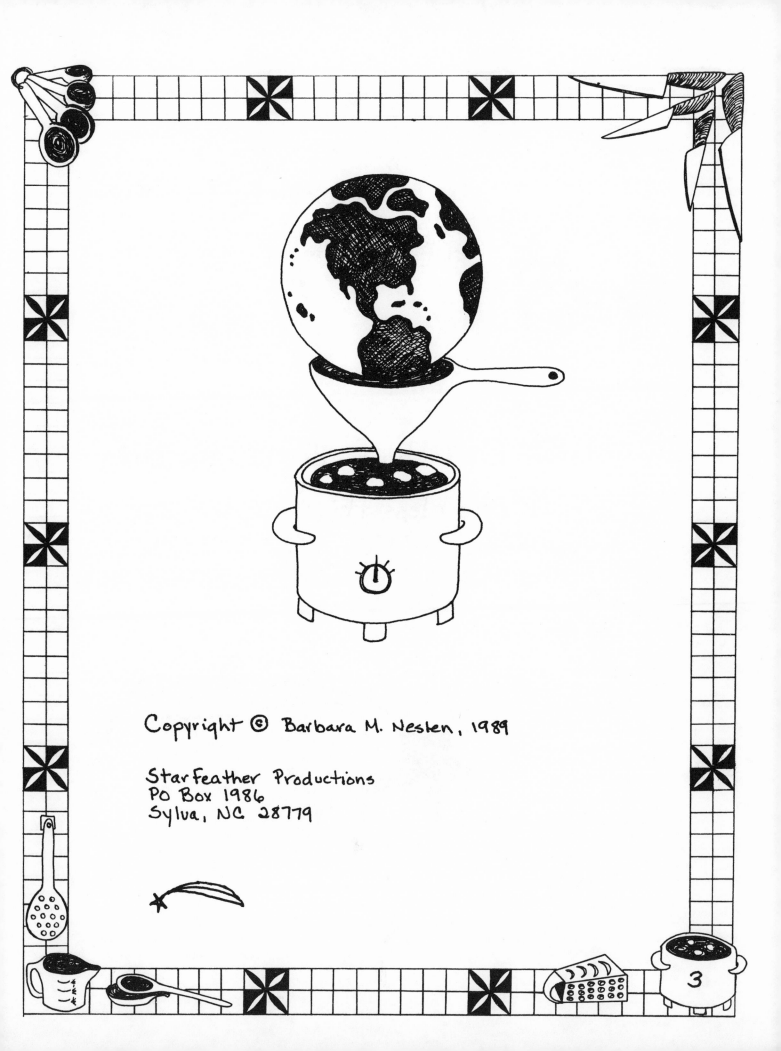

StarFeather Productions
PO Box 1986
Sylva, NC 28779

Oh God who feeds the little birds,
Please bless this food, this day.

4

Introduction

Cooking with a slow cooker is a hoot. You fill the crockery in the morning, and when it's dinner time and you're just getting home with tired feet and a full mind, feeling weather weary, facing an armload of paperwork, questioning kids needing time, a house needing care, and a hungry spouse, your house smells good and the food is done.

This book evolved out of love for friends who are just as busy as I, and whose time is just as valuable. They range from mothers busy with small children, schooling, volunteering, carpooling and puppeteering to the hardworking souls fighting the front lines of the business world. And I know there are many others out there (like yourself) whose lives are full and days seem to be speeding by. It takes so much time to think about, gather, prepare, serve and clean up food. (I didn't mention eating because that part goes all too fast in comparison with the rest). During the day I don't enjoy the nagging question in the back of my head, "What shall we have for dinner?" When I ask my family for suggestions, I always get: "What are my choices; I don't care - an attitude that changes as soon as the food is placed before them; steak and potatoes - I quit asking that budget-minded child; or Whatever you like." So we usually end up with, "Whatever is on sale; or Another Barbie surprise." And the funny thing is, they usually take just as long to prepare, if not longer, than filling the crockery and making a salad. Plus, I save the time and energy not worrying about what to eat. Crockery cooking helps you to get organized. It allows you to plan in advance and thereby take whatever you need out of the freezer the night before, make a shopping list, know when you'll have leftovers for lunch, or even plan an evening out.

I began meal planning when I got pregnant with my fourth child. My life was full of food at the time. I would fill 5 pots at least once a day. There was recording and measuring (a new experience when creating), gathering recipes, passing out new ones to try, timing and taste-testing. I had a lot of help from the people around me: my family, the Hospice training group, teachers, carpenters, fellow co-op members, the girls at the office, my PCI family, the staff at the A&P, three very special friends with healthy appetites, and Mary Sue, whose first impressions often turned into the recipe's name.

But when the morning sickness hit, I didn't want anything to do with food. I didn't want to smell it, touch it, cook it, clean up after it, or think about it, let alone eat it or write about it. Meal planning would mean I could spend the minimum time neccessary dealing with food to feed my family.

I hope this book can accomplish the same thing for others. So dig out that crockery you got as a wedding gift, or at the flea market and make it work for your lifestyle. It's a handy dandy kitchen tool.

(even if it won't pop popcorN)

For Your Information

I. General Information

A. The heat comes from the sides of the crockery; therefore....

    1. Scorching - eliminated

    2. Juices - retained

    3. Shrinkage - lessened

Save Money →   a. cheaper cuts - work well

    b. flavor - maintained

    4. Hard to overcook

B. When the crockery is on Low:

    1. Uses 75 watts

    2. Cooks at 200°, killing bacteria when 165° is maintained over 2 hours

C. When the crockery is on High:

    1. Uses 150 watts

Save Money →   2. Cooks at 300°, costing less than 8¢ a day to use, depending on where you live.

D. NEVER immerse crockery

E. All recipes are calculated for a 3½ quart crockery.

F. Each pot cooks a little different.

II. Handy Hints

A. ALWAYS FILL POT AT LEAST HALF FULL

B. Put vegetables on the bottom - they take longer to cook.

C. Cook overnight what you want for breakfast or to take along for lunch.

D. When in doubt, spray your crockery with a non-stick cooking spray.

E. You can connect the crockery to a timing device for a delayed start.

F. The crockery makes a great warmer.

G. To revive crackers or chips – place in the crockery on Low for 2 hours – no lid

H. To make gravy, try one of these:
  1. Mix together equal parts of flour and water and stir in slowly (start with 2/3 cup).
  2. Just add a can of cream of mushroom soup.
  3. Add cornstarch – 1 Tbsp per cup of liquid.
  4. Turn crockery on High and remove lid to thicken liquid.

I. A guideline to convert your favorite recipes:

350° x 1 hour = 6-8 hours on Low

300° x 30 minutes = 3-4 hours on Low

III My Personal Quirks

A. I never cook with pepper, so if you want it, you have to add it. (I'm allergic.)

B. I use minimum amounts of salt.

C. The garlic I love is minced in oil. It's easy and tasty. (3 cloves = 1 teaspoon)

D. I think of my crockery as a little ole' lady who stands around cooking for me all day.

    1. So I treat her with gentle, subtle temperature changes.

    2. I soak her in warm soapy water. It's the least I can do for her after she's worked hard for me all day. A friend deserves good treatment.

E. I wanted to calculate cooking and preparation times for you, but accuracy is difficult when my cooking time includes phone calls, diaper changes, visitors, hugging, dancing and help (especially the enthusiastic kind from a 1, 3, 5 & 7 year old)

F. Allison calculated serving amounts. After a few pots, you'll know if it will feed 6 hungry kids or 4 adults or both. A pot full can always feed my family of 6.

IV. Appreciation

A. Thanks Quayle for all the taste testing, putting up with the experimentation, and spurring me on.

B. An attitude of gratitude to Norm and Richard for perspective and Light.

C. Thanks to my kids Jenny, Emily, Martha, and George for their brave taste buds, willing spirits, and collective energy that created the need for this book.

D. Thank you Allene for being so willing and easy to work with.

E. Loving thanks to Joe, Jeff, and Allison for letting the laughter flow, the love grow, and the smiles sprout.

F. Special thanks to my friends whose divine timing keeps the Love spiraling upwards. You are a true treasure.

G. A heart full thank you to Mary Sue for all the many ways you helped. This book would not have been possible without you. I love you.

H. Ernie and Dru, a love that will last forever. And of course, Heather, too.

I. Thanks for the last minute help Deb.

J. Thanks for letting me share my heart.

P.S. I never liked the section in books called, "How To Use This Book."

13

How To Use This Book

Open to recipe, "bash" binding soundly, causing book to lie flat;
or....
Place book close to measuring, stirring, and pouring, thereby splashing pages, causing shriveling and crinkles, marking the recipe;
or....
Buy by the dozen, bind with string or very large rubber bands and us as a booster seat for small children.
Handy hint.... As the child grows, you can give the books away as gifts, and if they're close friends, they won't mind any spillage.
or....
Leave the book on the back of the toilet and thumb through it to an appealing recipe name. Try it. Then try the recipe before it and behind it. Do this three times;
or....

When face with a bumper crop, or a long freezer defrosting power failure, turn to the index, find your food, and experiment, or....

When doing your weekly / bimonthly meal planning, give yourself a break by using crockery cooking.

TABLE OF CONTENTS

Good Things To Get Up To
pages 20-31

cereals, eggs, fruit and more

Pour It In The Pot
pages 34-51

soups and stews

Eating Off The Range
pages 54-71

beef, pork, and lamb

Sunday Brunch
pages 74-87

poultry

Mexican Delights
pages 90-105

meat and beans assembled for delight

Veqies

pages 108-125

favorites from the vegetable kinqdom

For My Veqetarian Friends pages 128-145

qoodies, qrains, and tofu

Kids' Favorites

pages 148-167

pasta, casseroles, and desserts
(a few adult favorites too)

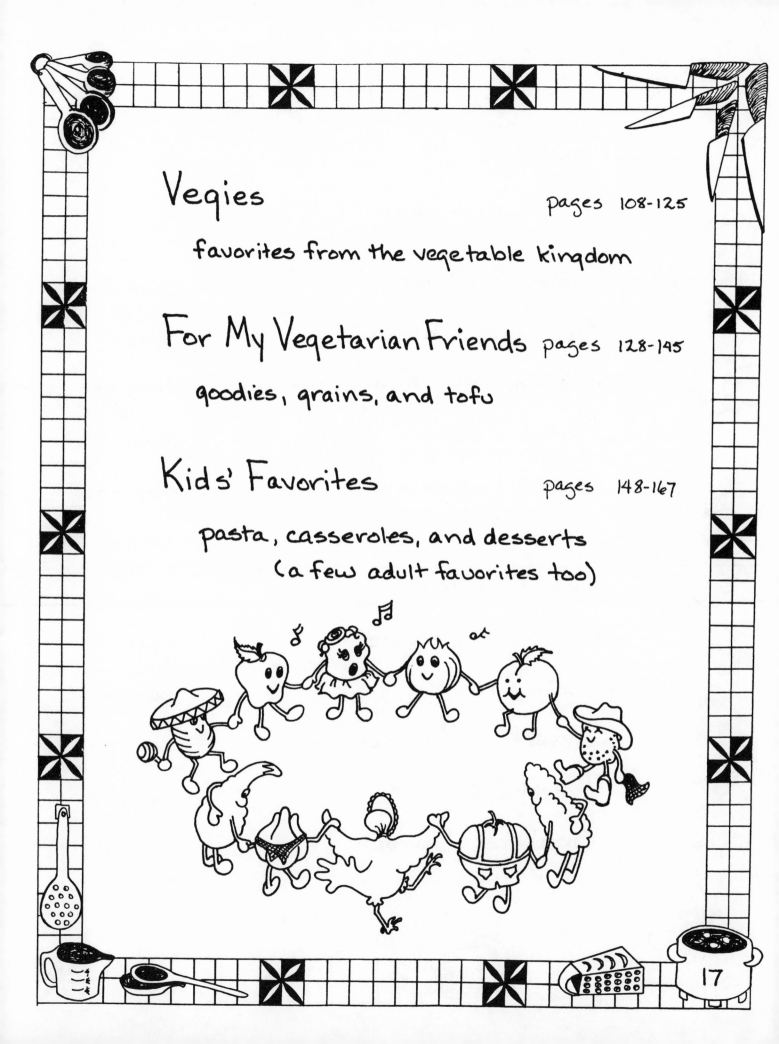

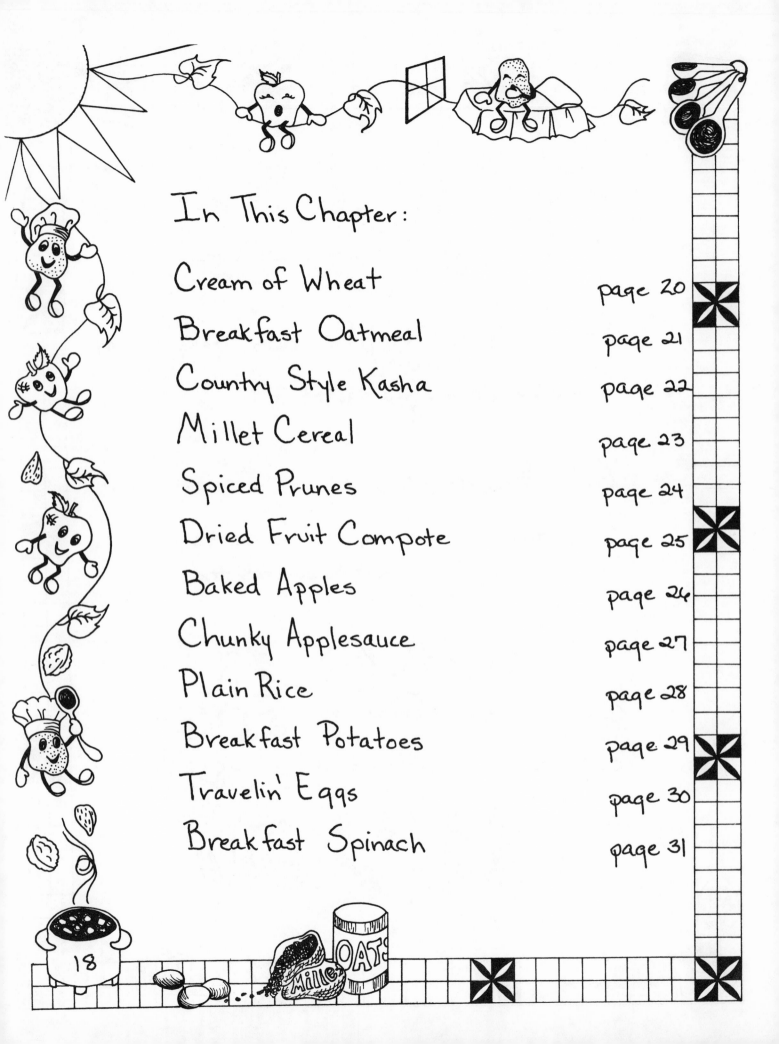

In This Chapter:

Cream of Wheat — page 20

Breakfast Oatmeal — page 21

Country Style Kasha — page 22

Millet Cereal — page 23

Spiced Prunes — page 24

Dried Fruit Compote — page 25

Baked Apples — page 26

Chunky Applesauce — page 27

Plain Rice — page 28

Breakfast Potatoes — page 29

Travelin' Eggs — page 30

Breakfast Spinach — page 31

Good Things To Get Up To

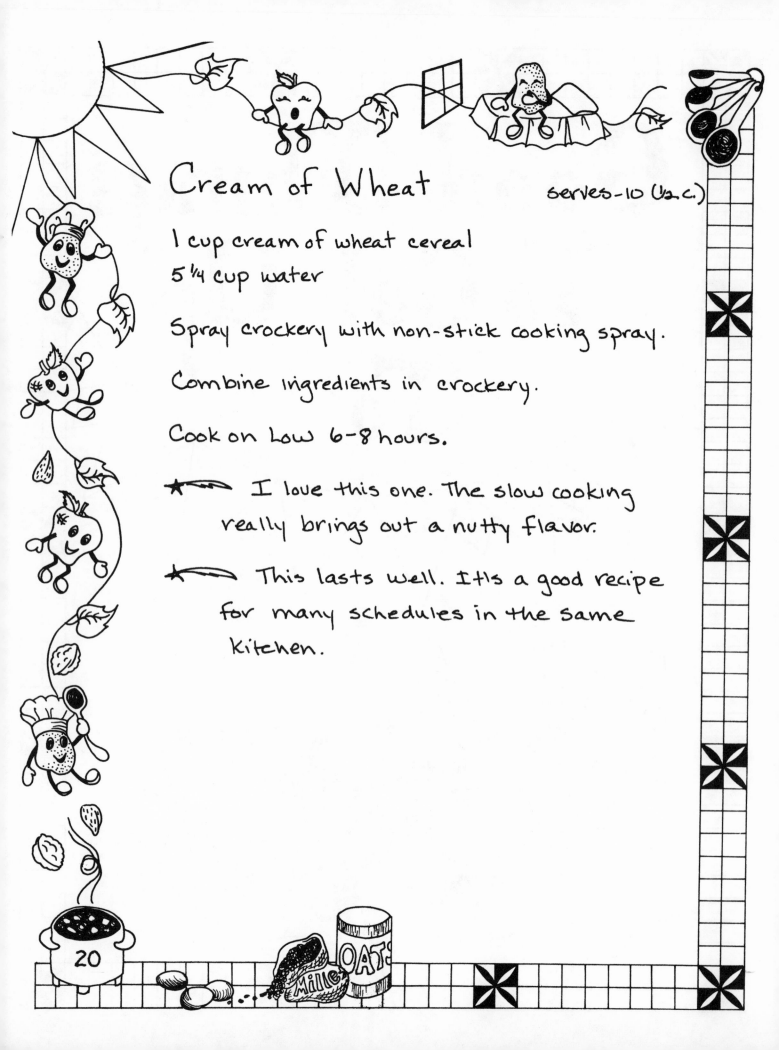

Cream of Wheat

serves-10 (½ c.)

1 cup cream of wheat cereal

5 ¼ cup water

Spray crockery with non-stick cooking spray.

Combine ingredients in crockery.

Cook on Low 6-8 hours.

★ I love this one. The slow cooking really brings out a nutty flavor.

★ This lasts well. It's a good recipe for many schedules in the same kitchen.

20

Breakfast Oatmeal

Serves 4 (½ cup)

1 cup oatmeal

2¼ cup water

⅓ cup raisins (optional)

Spray crockery with non-stick cooking spray.

Combine ingredients in crockery.

Cook on Low 8-10 hours.

* When the raisins cook with the oatmeal, it sweetens it - so adjust the amount of added sweetner.

* Other options: apples
cinnamon and nuts (I like almonds).
all of the above

* Each slow cooker cooks differently. You'll need to adjust the water and cooking time to find the right balance between mush and crunch.

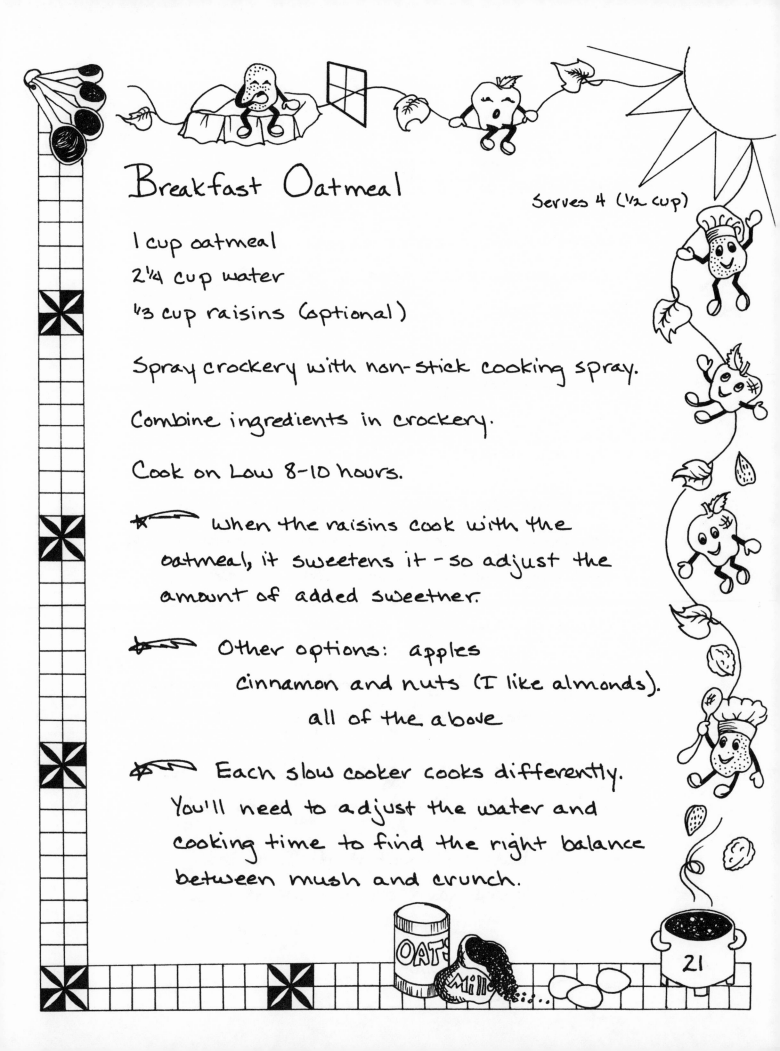

21

Country Style Kasha

1 egg, lightly beaten
1 cup buckwheat groats (kasha)
1/2 tsp salt
2 cups water
1/2 cup wheat germ
1/2 cup cottage cheese
1/2 cup yogurt

Combine egg, kasha, and salt and cook in dry saucepan until grains are separate and dry. Pour into crockery with water.

Cook on Low 6-8 hours.

Stir in wheat germ and top each bowl with cottage cheese and yogurt.

✱ This was quite a different taste and took a little getting used to for me.

✱ Kids will eat it if I added strawberry jam on top of the cottage cheese.

Millet Cereal

Serves 8 (1½ cup)

1 cup millet
3½ cup water
1 Tbsp margarine

Spray crockery with non-stick cooking spray. Combine ingredients in crockery.

Cook on Low 8-10 hours.

Dress like oatmeal:
1. margarine and salt
2. margarine and maple syrup
3. butter and brown sugar
4. milk can be added to any of the above.

★← Millet is a cereal grass whose small grain is used in Europe and Asia. It is used to make couscous.

★← I use the lefovers to make millet burgers. Just add an egg and enough flour to hold it together. Fry on both sides and serve on bread with mayo, mustard and sprouts.

23

Spiced Prunes

Serves 8 (½ cup)

1 pound dried prunes
4 cups water
2 slices orange
1 cinnamon stick
½ tsp vanilla

Place everything but vanilla into the crockery.

Cook on Low 6-8 hours (overnight).

Remove lid, turn off and stir in vanilla.
Serve lukewarm.

★ I like these with sprouted wheat toast.

★ Serve chilled with whipped cream for dessert.

Dried Fruit Compote

Serves 8 (1½ cup)

1 cup dried prunes

1 cup raisins

1 cup dried apricots

2½ cups apple juice

1 tsp lemon juice

Place all ingredients in your crockery. Stir.

Cook on Low 10-12 hours (overnight).

Serve chilled.

★ Keeps well for weeks in refrigerator.

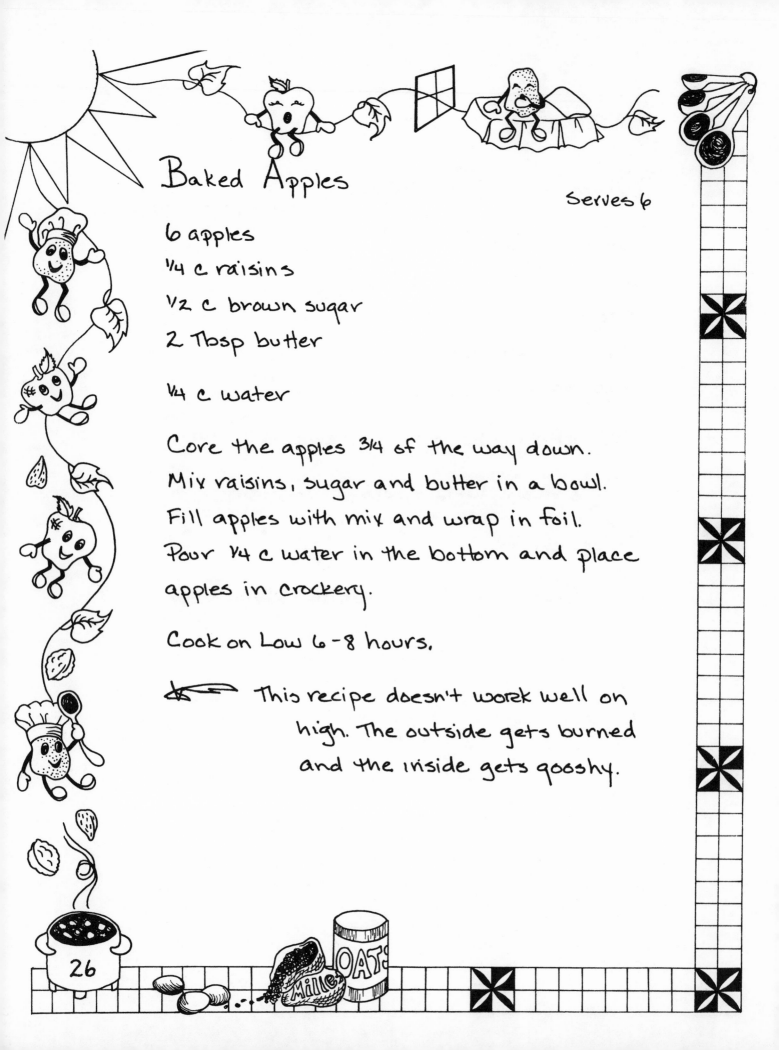

Baked Apples

Serves 6

6 apples
¼ c raisins
½ c brown sugar
2 Tbsp butter

¼ c water

Core the apples ¾ of the way down.
Mix raisins, sugar and butter in a bowl.
Fill apples with mix and wrap in foil.
Pour ¼ c water in the bottom and place apples in crockery.

Cook on Low 6-8 hours.

This recipe doesn't work well on high. The outside gets burned and the inside gets gooshy.

26

Chuncky Applesauce

Serves 6

8 apples
1/2 c water
1 tsp cinnamon
1/2 - 1 cup sugar or 1/2 c maple syrup

Peel and slice the apples in large chunks.
Stir together with the water and sweetner.
Pour into the crockery.

Cook on Low 8-10 hours,
    or High 3-4 hours.

★ In the fall I like to substitute red hots for the cinnamon and sugar.

★ The best baking apples are Courtlands, Staymans, Winesaps, Baldwins and Rome Beautys.

All-purpose apples that will work are Jonathan, Northern Spy, McIntosh, Gravenstein, and Rhode Island Greening

Don't use overripe apples.

Enjoy

OAT'S

27

Plain Rice

Serves 4 (½ cup)

2¼ c water

1 c. rice

Combine in the crockery.

Cook on Low 6-8 hours.

High 3-4 hours.

★ When cooked on High there will be crunchies on the side.

★ I serve plain rice:

1. For breakfast with soft boiled eggs
2. With steamed vegies and cheese sauce
3. With any of the available rice sauces

★ If it is too mushy for you, decrease the water to 2 cups.

★ For a change, I add a bouillon cube. Morga vegetable bouillon cubes are my favorite.

Breakfast Potatoes

Serves 6

4 potatoes
1 onion
4 oz cheese
1 Tbsp margarine
4 slices bacon

Slice the potatoes - peeling optional. Chop the onion. Grate the cheese and fry or microwave the bacon. Layer: Potatoes and margarine
onions
bacon
cheese
Repeat layers once.
Cook on Low 8-10 hours.

My kids love this in individual foil wrappers. It travels well that way too.

Travelin' Eggs

Serves 8 (½ cup)

2 c Bisquick

3/4 c ham-cubed

1 c swiss or cheddar cheese -grated

½ c onion - finely chopped

1/3 c parmesan cheese

1/3 c sour cream

2 Tbsp parsley

½ tsp salt

2 garlic cloves

2/3 c milk

6 eggs

Spray crockery with vegetable oil.

Mix all ingredients together in a bowl.

Pour into crockery.

Cook on Low 6-8 hours.

The more you eat... the better
it tastes.

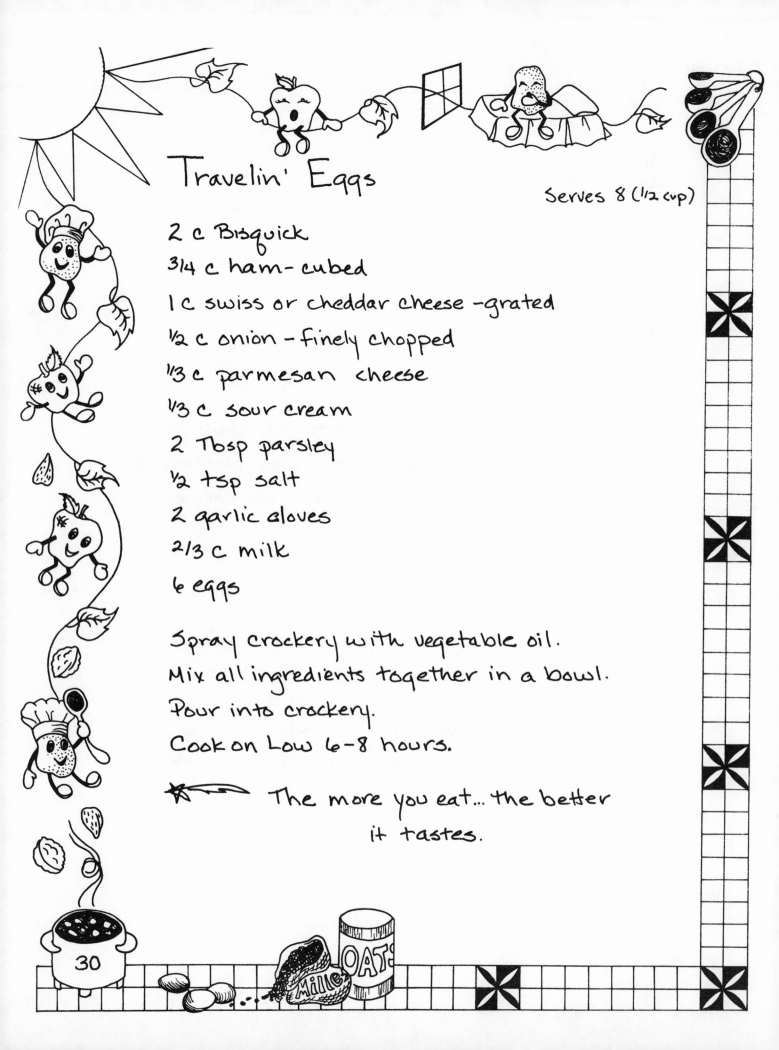

Breakfast Spinach

Serves 6 (1½ cup)

1 10 oz pkg frozen spinach - thawed and drained

1 cup Swiss cheese - grated

½ cup onion - chopped

1½ cup milk

3 eggs

¾ cup Bisquick

1 tsp salt

pinch nutmeg

Spray crockery with non-stick cooking spray.

Mix spinach, cheese and onion together in a bowl. Pour into crockery. Mix remaining ingredients in a blender and pour into crockery.

Cook on Low 10-12 hours

In This Chapter....

Good Ole Stew .... page 34

Refrigerator Stew .... page 35

Martha's Creation .... page 36

Meatball Stew .... page 37

Kat's Greek Stew .... page 38

Vegie Soup a la El .... page 39

Tortilla Soup .... page 40

Turkey Soup .... page 41

Steak Soup .... page 42

"A Little Bit Of This" Soup .... page 43

Patti's Potato Soup (Clam Chowder) .. page 44

Split Pea Soup .... page 45

Chick Pea Soup .... page 46

Lentil Soup .... page 47

Pea Beans .... page 48

Country Pintos .... page 49

Fritz's Chili .... page 50

Prisicilla's Chili .... page 51

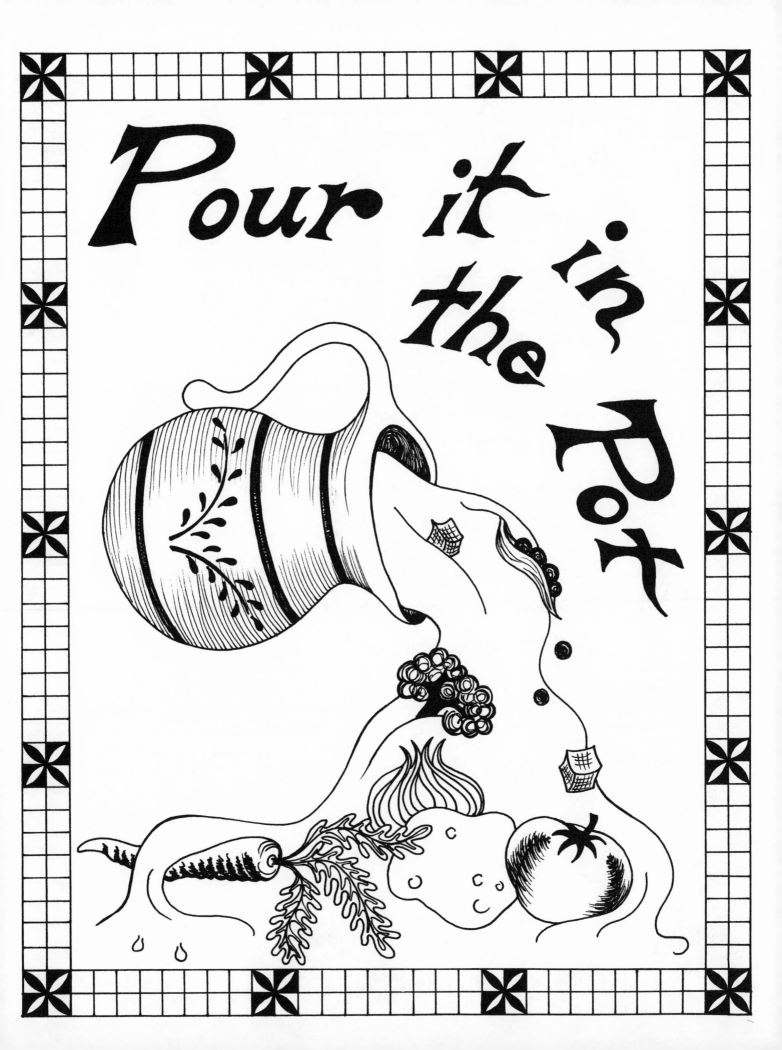

Good Ole Stew

Serves 6 (½ c)

2 pounds stew beef

6-8 carrots

3-4 potatoes

2 onions

1 can cream style corn

1 can tomato soup

1 cube beef bullion or 1 tsp granules

10 oz frozen peas (½ bag)

Cut meat and vegetables into large pieces.
Combine all ingredients (except peas) in
the crockery. Stir well.

Cook on Low 8-10 hours,

    High 3-4 hours.
   Add peas ½ hour before serving.

Refrigerator Stew

Serves 10 (½ c)

2 pounds beef stew

1 pkg onion soup mix

1 can cream of mushroom soup

1½ cups water

1 onion

4-6 carrots

3-4 potatoes

1 can green beans (15 oz)

1 can corn (15 oz)

Cut meat, onion, carrots and potatoes into bite size pieces. Combine all ingredients in the crockery. Stir well.

Cook on Low 8-10 hours.

★ I use this recipe to clean out the refrigerator. You can add anything, although tomatoes really change the taste.

★ I serve it with biscuits and fruit salad.

Enjoy

Martha's Creation

Serves 10

1 bag (1 pound) 15 beans

1 can stewed tomatoes

1 large onion - chopped

¼ pound mushrooms - sliced thick

2-3 stalks celery - chopped

3-4 carrots - sliced

enough water to cover ingredients

¼ lb bacon

½ tsp pick a pepper

3 cloves of garlic

Sauté bacon until starts to brown. Drain. Combine all ingredients in your crockery.

Cook on Low 8-10 hours.

⟵ 15 beans is a combination of dried beans that can be purchased in your local market. It should be with the pintos and split peas.

Meatball Stew

serves 8

Meatballs:

1 pound ground beef
1 Tbsp parsley
1 egg
½ tsp celery salt
¼ tsp dill weed

Stew Fixin's

½ med bell pepper - cut up
1 onion - chopped
2 cups whole tomatoes
½ tsp salt
12 oz red kidney beans
4 oz macaroni

Parboil macaroni 4 minutes. Form meatballs and brown in a skillet. Remove and drain. Add onion and bell pepper to skillet and sauté 2-3 minutes. Combine all ingredients in crockery.

Cook on Low 6-8 hours.

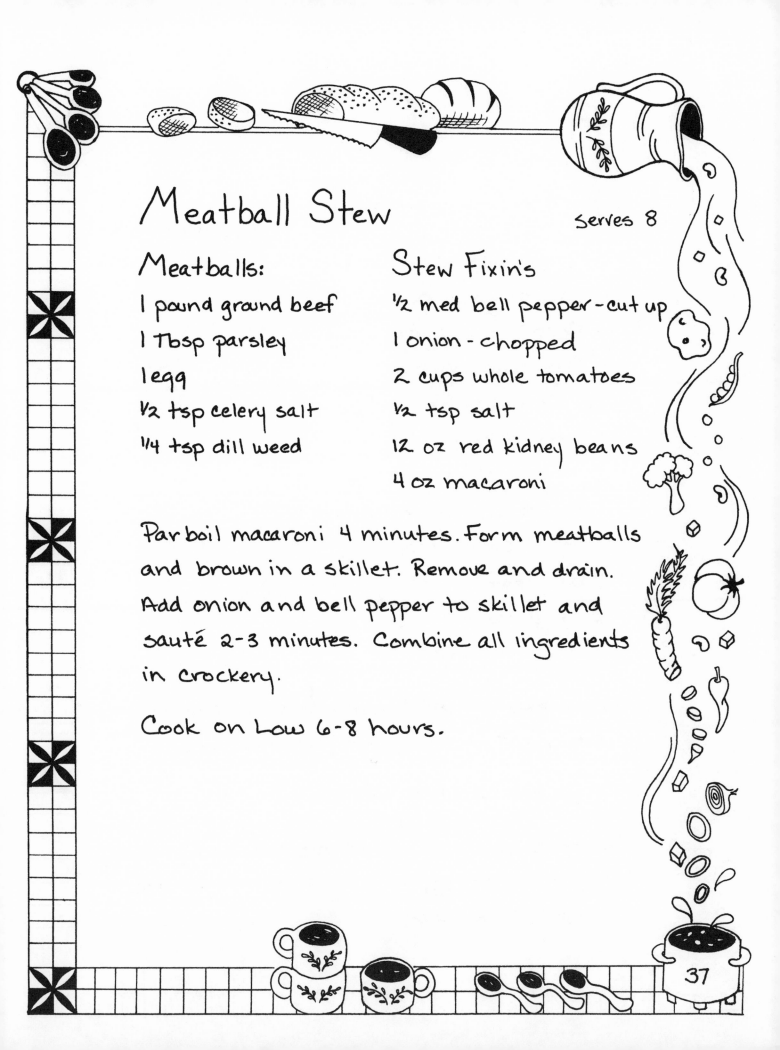

Kat's Greek Stew

Serves 9 (3oz)

1-2 pounds stew beef
1 can tomato paste
1 Tbsp brown sugar
1 Tbsp wine vinegar
½ cup red wine
½ tsp cumin
3 garlic cloves
1 tsp each salt and pepper
1 stick cinnamon
1 bay leaf
2 Tbsp raisins
2-3 whole cloves

Mix together all ingredients (except meat).
Add meat and pour into the crockery.

Cook on Low 6-8 hours

★— I don't consume alcohol, so I
substitute apple juice in recipes where
wine is needed.

Vegie Soup a la El

Serves 6 (½ c)

1 pound stew beef
1 turnip - diced
1 onion - diced
3 stalks celery - chopped
5 cups water

2 potatoes - diced
3 carrots - sliced
1 tomato - chopped
1 can (15oz) stewed tomatoes
½ pkg (½ pound) mixed garden vegetables

The night before:

Combine the first 5 ingredients in your crockery.
Cook overnight on Low (6-10 hours).

In the morning:
Add the rest of the ingredients and stir well.
Cook on Low 6-8 hours.

★⟶ Always better the second day.

Tortilla Soup

Serves 8 (1 cup)

6 corn tortillas - cut into strips

½ cup oil

1 onion - minced

1 quart tomatoes - purée with the oil in blender

6 hard boiled eggs - chopped small

½ tsp cumin

1 tsp minced garlic in oil (3 cloves)

1 bay leaf

1 tsp oregano

1 tsp salt

4 oz cheddar cheese - grated

Combine all ingredients into crockery.

Cook on Low 6-8 hours.

I like to garnish with sour cream and some chopped green onions.

Oh boy, are you going to like this one.

Turkey Gumbo Soup

Serves 14 (1 cup)

4 cups turkey in bite size pieces

¼ pound ham - cubed

1½ cups onion - diced

1 cup green pepper - diced

1 cup celery - diced

⅓ cup rice

3 Tbsp flour

3 Tbsp oil

1 can okra with juice

1 quart canned tomatoes - mashed

1 jar (4oz) pimentos

2 bay leaves

3 cups water

Sauté ham, onions, peppers, celery in oil. Add rice and flour and stir 3-4 minutes. Combine everything in the crockery.

Cook on Low 8-10 hours.

★— Thanks, Eleanor

Steak Soup

Serves 6 (1cup)

1 pound steak (I use round) - cubed

2 sticks oleo (1/2 lb margarine)

1 cup flour

4 cups water

1/2 tsp salt

1 can (4oz) green beans

1 can (8oz) tomatoes

4 Tbsp beef granules
or
6 bullion cubes (beef)

2 large carrots - sliced

2 onions - diced

2 potatoes - diced

2 stalks celery - diced

1/2 pound frozen peas

Brown meat in 1/2 stick oleo. Remove meat and set aside. Melt rest of oleo in the same pan. Add flour to make a paste. Slowly add 2 cups water. Add rest of ingredients (except peas). Don't forget remaining 2 cups of water.

Cook on Low 8-10 hours.

Add peas the last 1/2 hour and adjust water.

★↝ This recipe always turns out slightly different each time.

"A Little Bit Of This" Soup

Serves 10 (1 cup)

1 can (1 lb 3 oz) ready-to-serve vegetable soup

1 can (10 ¾ oz) condensed soup - vegetable

1 cup tomato juice

4 potatoes

4 carrots

1 small onion

2 tomatoes

2 stalks of celery

2 yellow squash

1 can (8 oz) corn

1 can (8 oz) green beans

optional: 1 green pepper - diced

          1 cup diced pumpkin

Chop all vegetables into small pieces.

Combine all ingredients in the crockery.

Cook on Low 4-6 hours,

      High 3-4 hours.

The smaller the pieces, the faster it cooks.

Patti's Potato Soup

Serves 4 (1 cup)

2 cups potatoes
1½ cups onions
4 cups water
1½ tsp sea salt
2 Tbsp butter

Peel potatoes if so desired and dice.
Slice onions. Combine all ingredients
in the pot except the butter.

Cook on Low 8-10 hours,
       High 4-5 hours.

Add butter and serve.

✳ To make a thicker and creamier
soup, run it through the blender.

✳ To make Great Clam Chowder,
just add 3 (6½ oz) cans of clams.

Split Pea Soup

2 c split peas
6 c water
1 ham hock
1 large onion-chopped

Combine all ingredients in the crockery.

Cook on Low 8-12 hours.

Drain the soup through a colander - rubbing
with a spoon to help the thick part go
through. Remove bone and return any
edible pieces of meat to the soup.
Salt to taste. I like to run it through a blender.

☞ Be sure to rinse dishes and utensils
right away. Split pea soup is difficult to
clean when dry.

☞ If you have difficulty with gas-
cook two large carrots in the soup, then
discard.

Chick Pea Soup

Serves 6 (1 cup)

1 pound garbonzo beans (chick peas)

1/4 lb salt pork

1 large onion - chopped

2 garlic cloves - minced

1/4 c oil

6 c water

salt and pepper to taste

Combine all ingredients in the crockery.

Cook on Low 8-10 hours.

Serve as is or run it through a blender.

Lentil Soup

Serves 6 (1 cup)

½ pound lentils

6 cups water

1 small onion, chopped

2 cloves garlic, minced

½ cup tomato sauce

¼ cup oil

salt and pepper to taste

3 slices bacon, cut into small pieces

Rinse the lentils. Combine all ingredients in crockery.

Cook on Low 8-10 hours.

Pea Beans

Serves 8 (1 cup)

2 cups great northern beans (small white)

1 cup yellow split peas

8 cups water

1 ham hock or bone

2 cloves garlic-minced

2 Tbsp parsley

2 bay leaves

Rinse beans in hot water.

Combine all ingredients in the crockery.

Cook on Low 6-8 hours.

Remove meat source. Debone and return meat to crockery. Stir and serve.

Country Pintos

Serves 5 (1 cup)

1 pound pinto beans
5 cups water
2 oz salt pork

Combine in crockery and stir.

Cook on Low 10-12 hours.

The longer they cook, the better they are. Check water after 4-6 hours and add 1-2 cups as needed.

* I usually serve with Texas Cornbread.
* Tato loves them with green beans, slaw and a thick slice of onion.
* A Southern favorite is to serve them with mash potatoes, onion, weenies and sauerkraut.
* "A Poor Man's Supper" is used as a fund raiser. It's pintos, slaw and cornbread.

Fritz's Chili

Serves 8 (1 cup)

1½ pounds ground chuck
1 pkg chili seasoning mix
1 large onion - chopped
3 cans (16 oz) chili beans with gravy
1 can (16 oz) whole tomatoes - mashed
1 can (16 oz) red kidney beans
1-5 jalapeño peppers finely chopped (optional)

In a skillet, brown meat. Drain. Add meat with remaining ingredients, except peppers, into crockery and stir well.

Cook on Low 8-10 hours
High 3-4 hours

Before serving stir in jalapeños if desired.

Is your crockery plugged in?

Is it turned on?

Priscilla's Chili

Serves 8 (1 cup)

1 pound lean ground beef
½ pound Italian hot sausage
1 can (8 oz) tomatoes - mashed or squeezed
1 medium onion - diced
1 pkg chili seasoning mix
2 cans (15 oz) pinto beans
½ pound Monterey Jack or Longhorn cheese
diced onion

Brown meat with onion. Add seasonings
and stir. Stir in tomatoes. Pour beans
in crockery and add meat mixture. Stir well.

Cook on Low 6-8 hours.

Serve with grated cheese and the diced
    onion.

Thanks, Marty

51

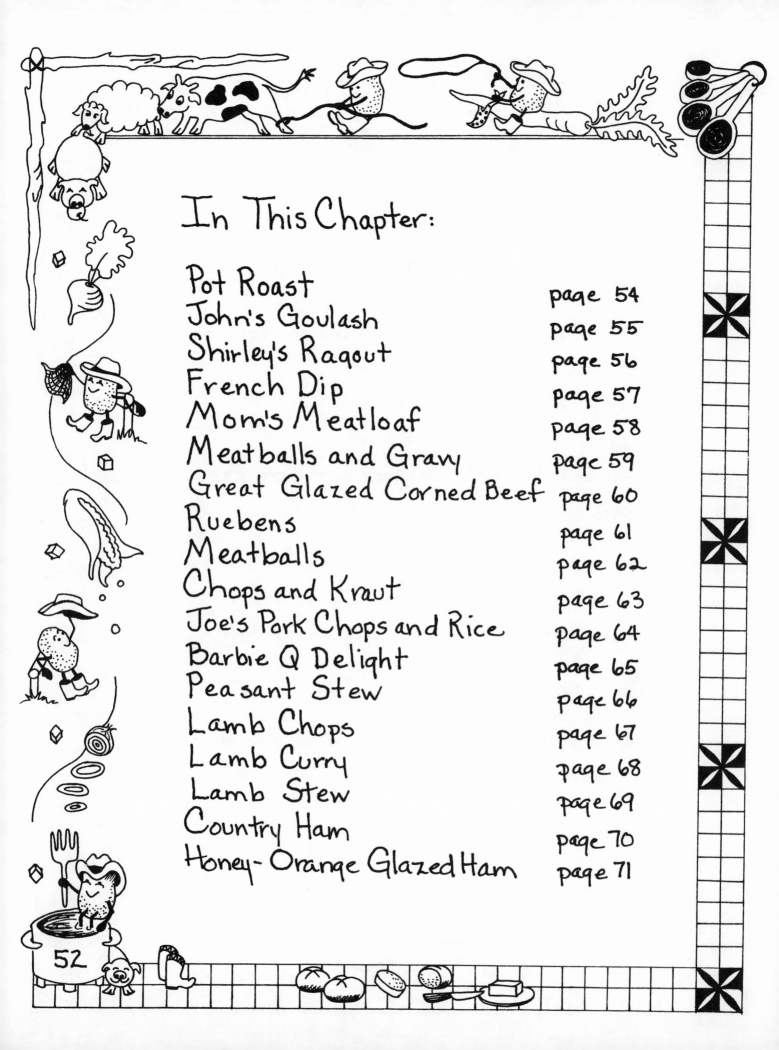

In This Chapter:

Pot Roast — page 54
John's Goulash — page 55
Shirley's Ragout — page 56
French Dip — page 57
Mom's Meatloaf — page 58
Meatballs and Gravy — page 59
Great Glazed Corned Beef — page 60
Ruebens — page 61
Meatballs — page 62
Chops and Kraut — page 63
Joe's Pork Chops and Rice — page 64
Barbie Q Delight — page 65
Peasant Stew — page 66
Lamb Chops — page 67
Lamb Curry — page 68
Lamb Stew — page 69
Country Ham — page 70
Honey-Orange Glazed Ham — page 71

Pot Roast

Serves 8

- 2-3 pound roast
- 3-4 carrots
- 2-3 potatoes
- 1-2 onions
- 1 pkg mushroom-onion soup mix

Place vegetables in the bottom of the crockery.
Peeling the carrots is optional. Skin the onions.
Place meat in next and top with soup.

Cook on Low 8-10 hours.
High 4-6 hours.

★ You can thicken the juices by adding cornstarch. The ratio is 1 Tbsp cornstarch per cup of liquid....
Or add a can of cream of mushroom soup.

John's Goulash

Serves 8

2-3 pounds stew beef
3 potatoes - diced
4 carrots - sliced
2 onions - diced
1 can (16oz) stewed tomatoes
1 can (16oz) tomato sauce
1 can (16oz) kidney beans
salt to taste

Combine all the ingredients in the crockery.

Cook on Low 6-8 hours

★ This is really good

★ Kids like it served over macaroni
   or noodles

Enjoy

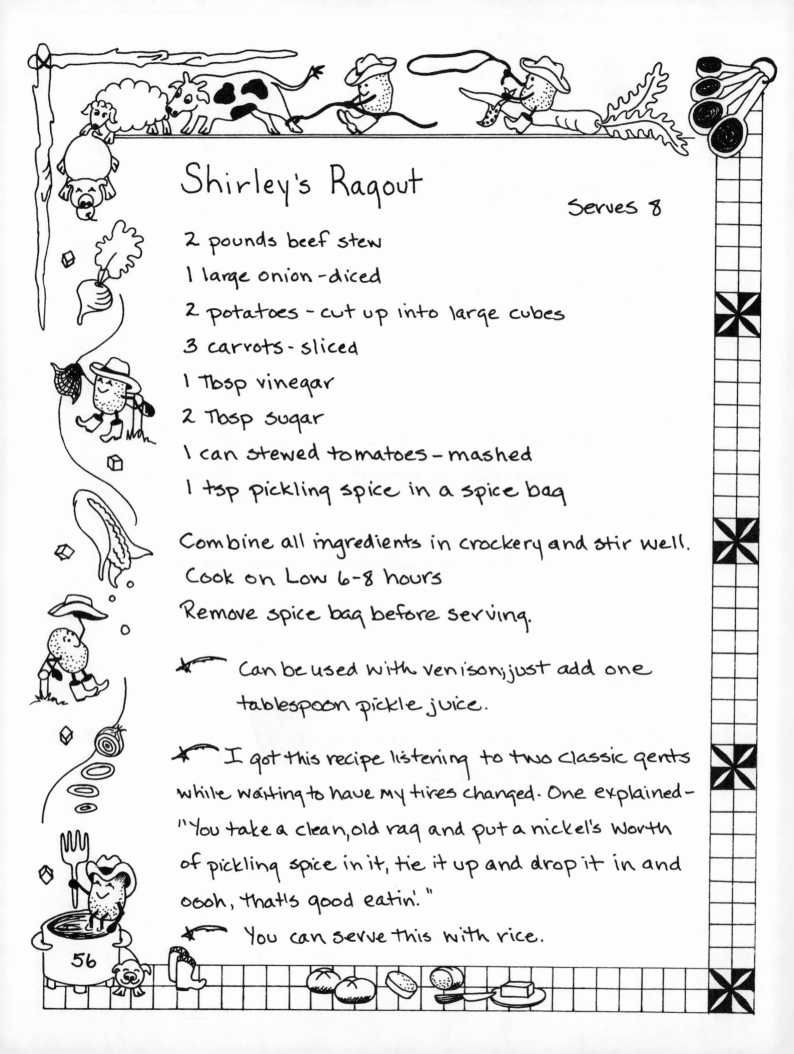

Shirley's Ragout

Serves 8

2 pounds beef stew

1 large onion - diced

2 potatoes - cut up into large cubes

3 carrots - sliced

1 Tbsp vinegar

2 Tbsp sugar

1 can stewed tomatoes - mashed

1 tsp pickling spice in a spice bag

Combine all ingredients in crockery and stir well.

Cook on Low 6-8 hours

Remove spice bag before serving.

⋆ Can be used with venison; just add one tablespoon pickle juice.

⋆ I got this recipe listening to two classic gents while waiting to have my tires changed. One explained - "You take a clean, old rag and put a nickel's worth of pickling spice in it, tie it up and drop it in and oooh, that's good eatin'."

⋆ You can serve this with rice.

French Dip

Serves 12

3 pound chuck roast

1 can (10 oz) beef broth or 1 tsp bullion in 1 cup water

1 pkg onion-mushroom soup mix

French rolls

Cut meat to fit crockery. Combine the dry soup and broth. Pour over meat.

Cook on High 6-8 hours

Remove meat with a slotted spoon to remove bones and any large fat. Replace meat in crockery and use a potato masher to separate meat. There should be more liquid than meat. If not, add more water or broth.

To make sandwiches - cut french rolls in half lengthwise and dip both sides in juices. Squirt mustard on one side, if desired, put meat on the other side and close. It's messy but delicious.

* Leftovers make a great soup stock.

☞ This is a good one.

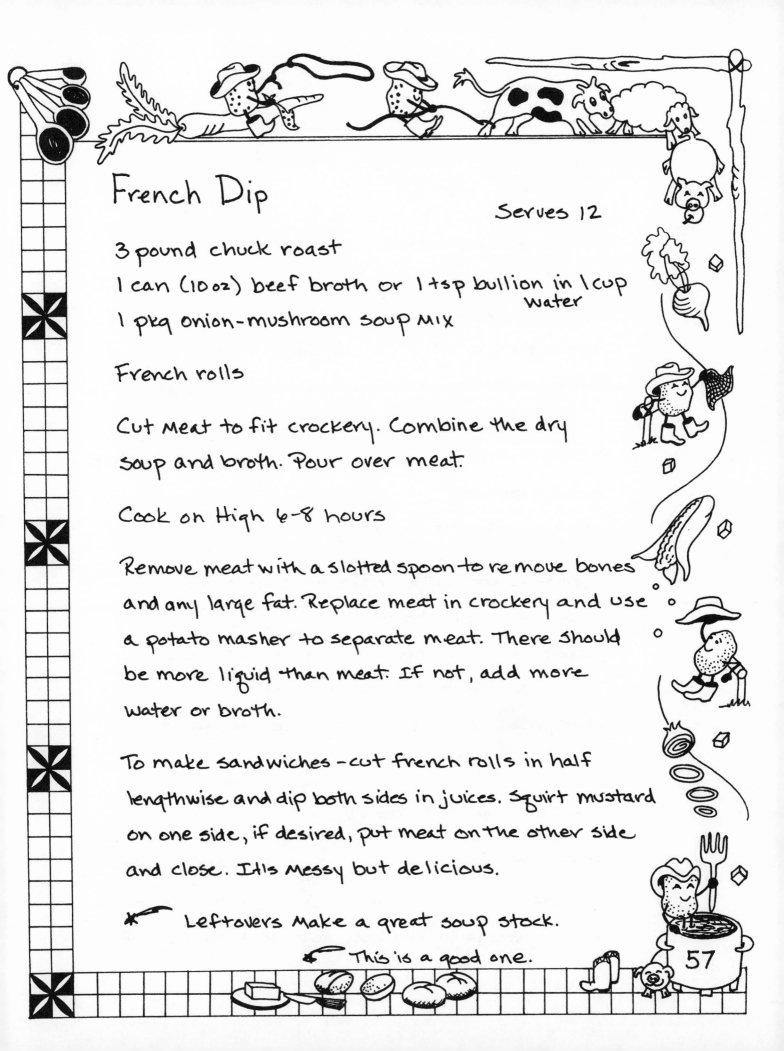

57

Mom's Meatloaf

Serves 6

1½ pounds ground chuck

1 small onion diced

1 slice of bread toasted

½ cup milk

2 eggs

½ tsp sage

3 Tbsp ketchup

2 Tbsp parsley

2 tsp worchestershire

Sauce:

½ cup ketchup

1 Tbsp brown sugar

1 tsp prepared mustard

Spray crockery with non-stick cooking oil.

Break up toast into milk.

Combine meat, onions, eggs and spices.

Add milk and toast and mix well.

Pour into crockery. Mix sauce ingredients
in a bowl and pour on top.

Cook on Low 4-6 hours.

I have to admit I prefer this baked
in a 350° oven for an hour, but I love the recipe
and wanted it in the book to have it handy-dandy.

Meatballs with Gravy

Serves 6

1-1½ pounds ground chuck

2 Tbsp parsley

1 tsp Lawry's Seasoning salt

¼ cup bread crumbs

¼ cup milk

2 Tbsp cornstarch

1 pkg gravy mix

Combine first 5 ingredients to make walnut-size meatballs. Brown them in a saucepan. Place in crockery on Low. In another pan add gravy mix and cornstarch to 1 cup cold water. Stir and bring to a boil. Add to drippings in saucepan and stir, stir, stir. . Pour over meatballs.

Cook on Low 3-4 hours.   It will keep all day.

✱ I usually serve it with rice, cooked carrots, and lime Jello with cottage cheese & pineapple.

✱ My kids love it - hope you do too.

✱ Thanks, Alice

Great Glazed Corned Beef

Serves 10

5 pound corned beef

2 bay leaves

Glaze:

3 Tbsp melted margarine	1/3 cup ketchup
1 Tbsp prepared mustard	3 Tbsp vinegar
1/3 cup brown sugar	3 Tbsp water

The night before:

Place meat in crockery. Cut to fit if needed.

Cover with water and add bay leaves.

Cook overnight on Low 6-10 hours.

In the morning:

Drain off liquid, reserving to cook vegies.

In a sauce pan heat glaze ingredients,

stirring until blended. Pour over meat.

Cook on Low 6-8 hours.

★ If you have a second pot, fill it with
the reserve liquid, carrots, potatoes,
onions and cabbage.   Yummy.

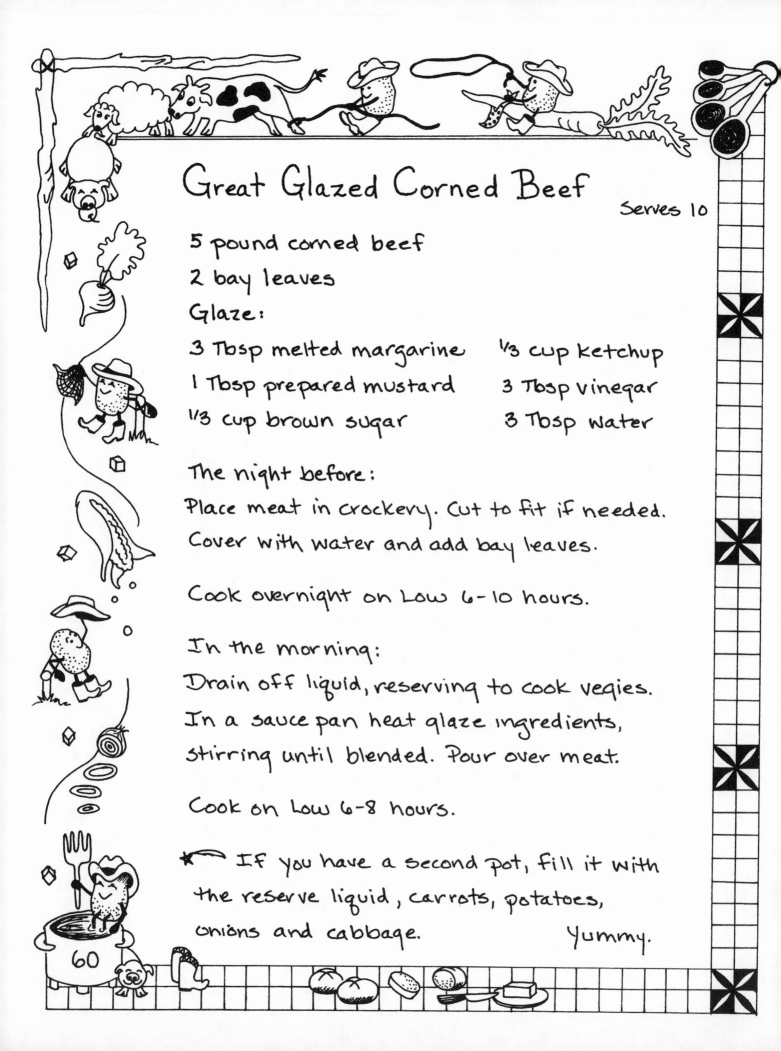

60

Ruebens

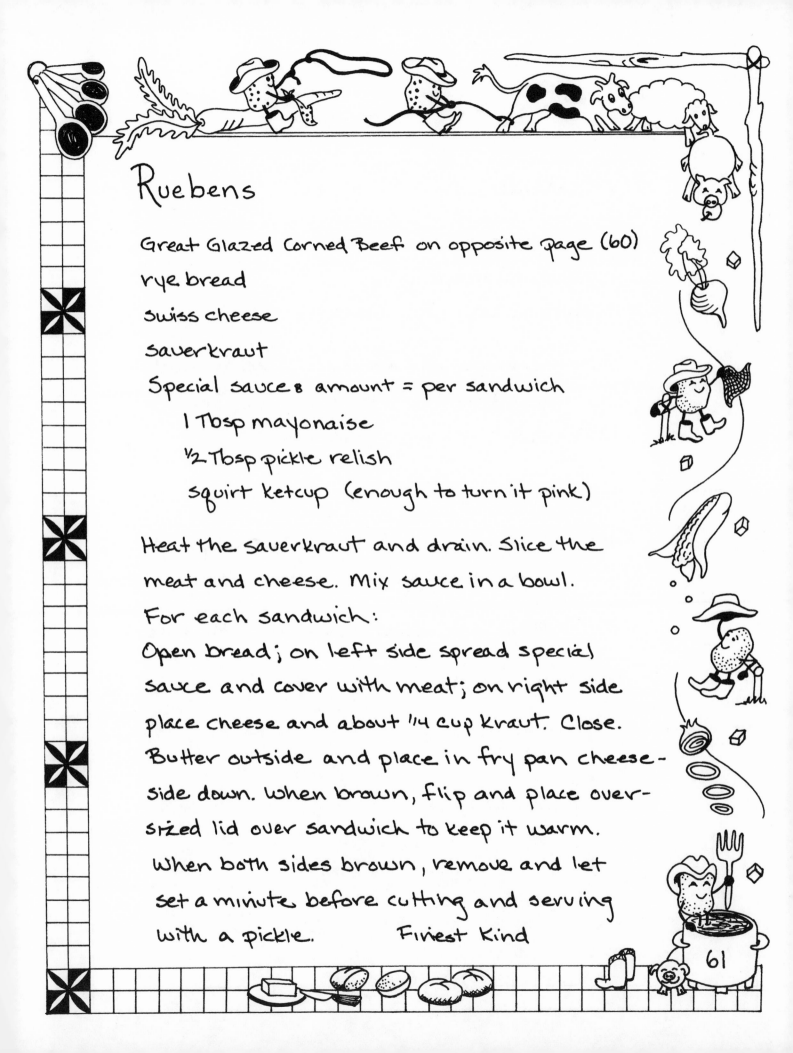

Great Glazed Corned Beef on opposite page (60)

rye bread

Swiss cheese

Sauerkraut

Special sauce: amount = per sandwich

  1 Tbsp mayonaise

  ½ Tbsp pickle relish

  squirt ketcup (enough to turn it pink)

Heat the sauerkraut and drain. Slice the meat and cheese. Mix sauce in a bowl.
For each sandwich:
Open bread; on left side spread special sauce and cover with meat; on right side place cheese and about ¼ cup kraut. Close. Butter outside and place in fry pan cheese-side down. When brown, flip and place over-sized lid over sandwich to keep it warm. When both sides brown, remove and let set a minute before cutting and serving with a pickle.   Finest Kind

Meatballs

Serves 6-8

1-1½ pounds ground chuck
1 jar (16oz) grape jelly
1 bottle (12oz) chili sauce

Combine grape jelly and chili sauce in crockery. Form ground meat into balls and drop in. Stir well to coat the meatballs.

Cook on Low 6-8 hours.

★ This one is fun to take to a party and have the guest guess the ingredients.

★ These are sweet - popular with kids.

★ Thanks, Mom

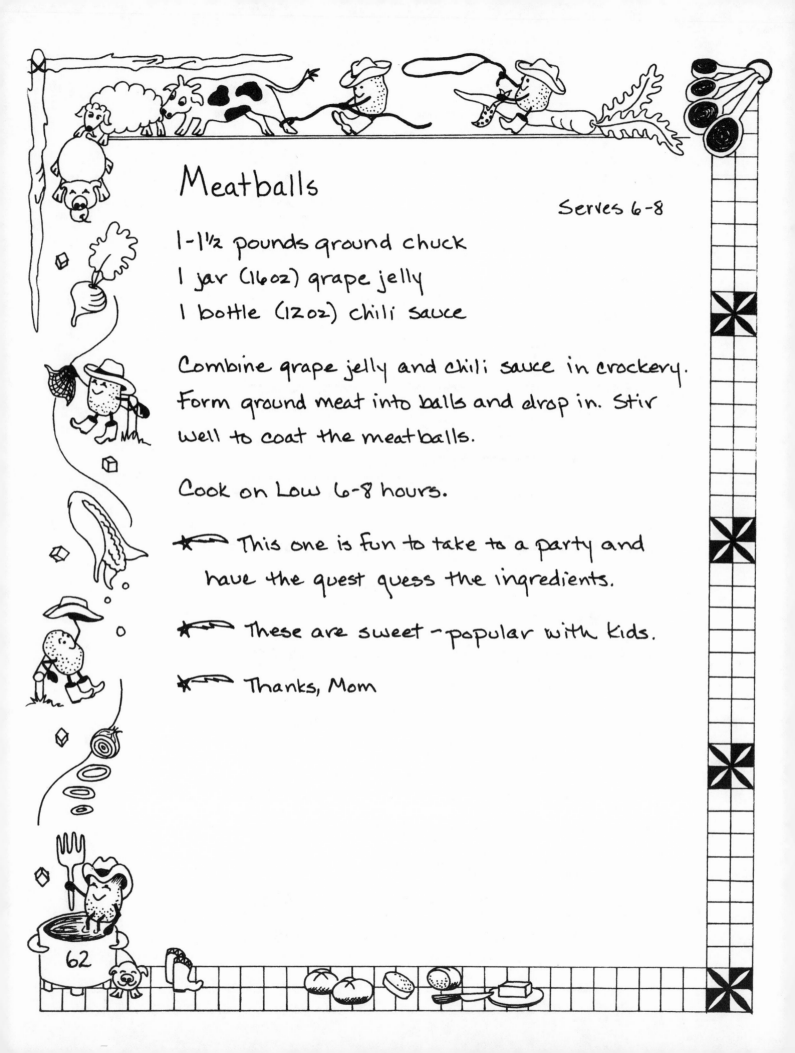

Chops and Kraut

Serves 6

6-8 pork chops
2 large onions - sliced
1 pound bag of sauerkraut

Layer in crockery -
      a little kraut, onion, pork chop
          another layer
             until all is gone in.

Cook on Low 6-8 hours.

Serve with applesauce.

Thanks, Diane

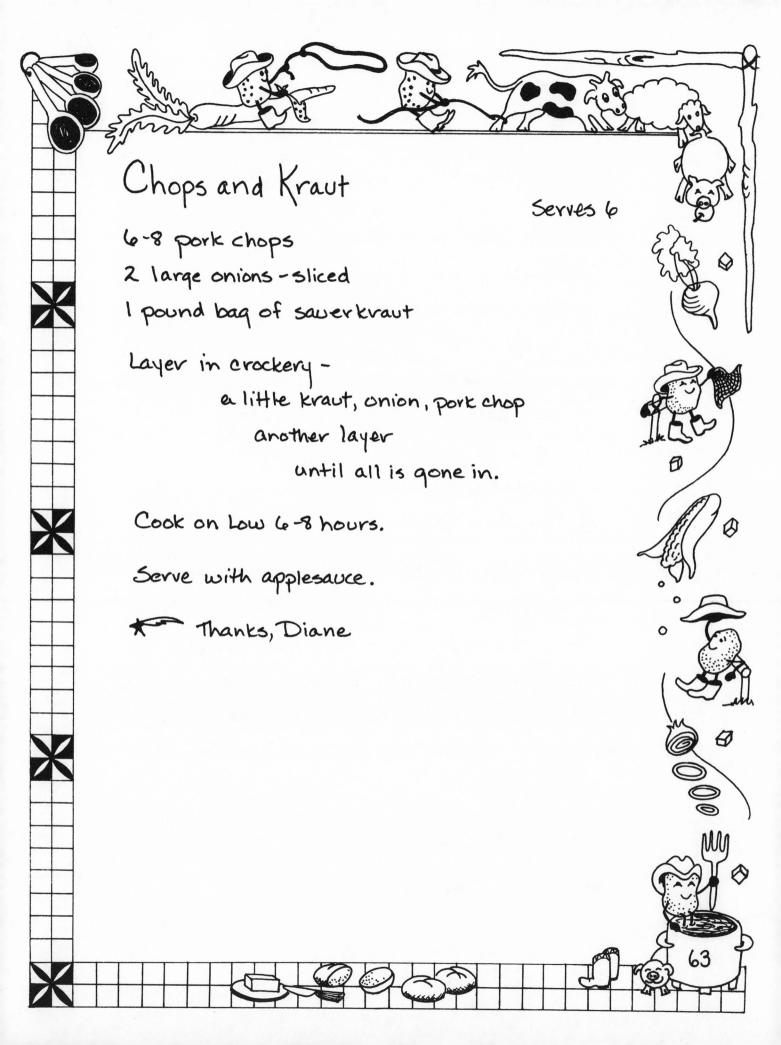

Joe's Pork Chops and Rice

Serves 4

4 thick sliced pork chops

2 apples

1 cup brown rice

1 onion - diced

1 tsp parsley

1 stalk celery with leaves - diced

1 tsp salt

1 cup hot water

1/2 tsp chili powder

Combine everything but the pork chops and apples in the crockery. Stir well. Core the apples and slice each one making four rings. Place on top of the rice. Brown the chops on each side to help seal in the flavor. Place on top of the apples.

Cook on Low 6-8 hours.

Thanks, Jeff

Barbie Q Delight

Serves 6-8

2 cups of your favorite bar-b-que sauce

1 whole chicken or favorite parts cut up

or.... a pork tender loin

or.... beef or pork ribs

or.... 2 pounds tofu - sliced

Place your choice in the crockery and cover with sauce.

Cook on Low 6-8 hours.

✱ I like to preboil the ribs, in a separate pan about 10 minutes to help reduce fat and tenderize.

✱ My absolute favorite bar-b-que sauce is: BARTOW'S BAR-B-QUE on Hwy 441 between Tallulah Falls and Clayton, Ga.

✱ Thanks, Dan and Alice

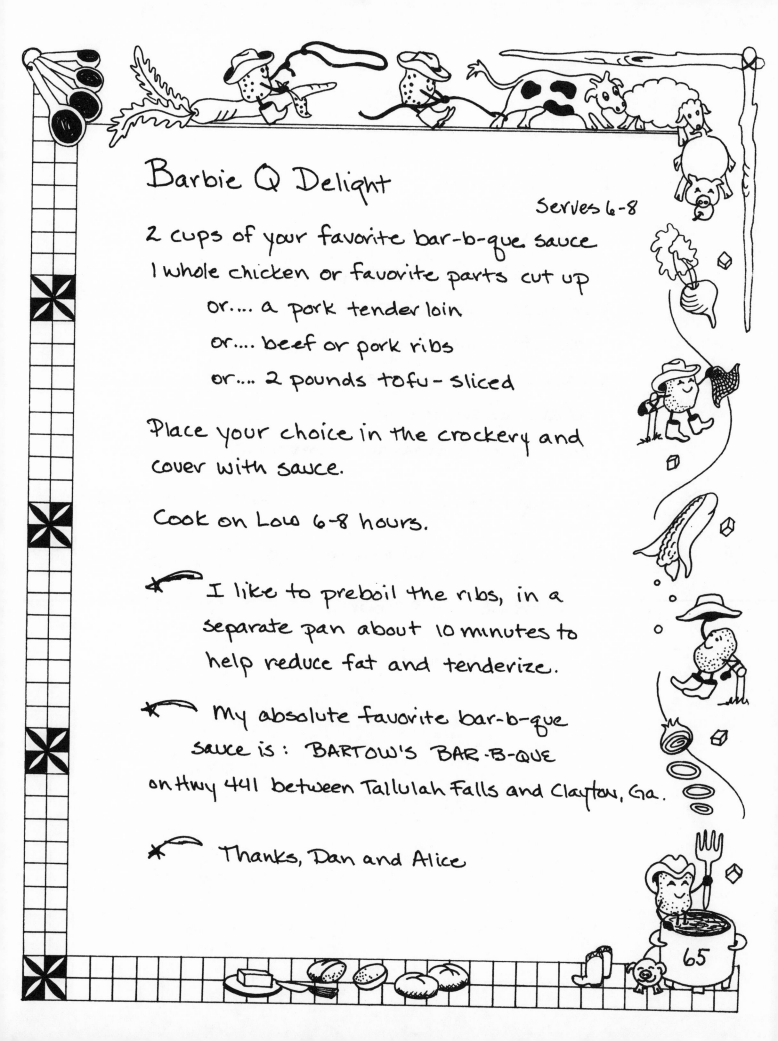

Peasant Stew

Serves 8

3 cups lamb cubes

3/4 cup Italian dressing

1 envelope onion soup mix

4 carrots- sliced

1 can (10oz) green beans with juice

3 stalks celery -sliced

1 can (10½oz) creamy onion soup

The night before - marinate meat in refrigerator.

Combine all ingredients in crockery.

Cook on Low 6-8 hours.

Serve with biscuits.

Lamb Chops

Serves 4

4 lamb chops
1 pkg onion soup mix
roaster bag

1 cup barley
2 cups water
1 onion - diced
1 tsp salt

Place the chops in the roaster bag and pour the soup mix on top. Inflate bag, twisting top to hold air and shake to coat the chops. Roll down the top of the bag, poke 3-4 holes in it. Mix the rest of the ingredients in the crockery and place the bag on top.

Cook on Low 8 hours.

★ If you want the flavors to blend poke the holes in the bottom of the bag. If not, poke the holes in the top of the bag.

★ You can use the leftover barley for soups, and stews and salads.

Lamb Curry

Serves 8

¼ pound margarine
1 large onion -diced
2 garlic cloves - minced
1 Tbsp parsley
1 stalk celery - diced
1 bay leaf
¼ tsp dry mustard
1 tart apple, peeled and diced
2 Tbsp flour
½ tsp mace
2 tsp curry powder
1½ cups chicken broth
2 cups cooked lamb - cubed

Sauté in margarine, the onion, garlic, parsley, celery, bay, mustard and apple. Add flour, mace and curry. Pour into crockery and add broth. Stir well. Add meat and stir again. Cook on Low 6-8 hours.
Serve over noodles.

Lamb Stew

Serves 6

3 cups lamb - cubed
½ cup French dressing
½ cup Catalina dressing
1 large onion - diced
3 carrots - sliced
2 cups mashed potatoes
1 cup water

Combine all ingredients except potatoes in crockery. Top with a ring of potatoes.

Cook on Low 6-8 hours.

Stir and serve.

← This is great!

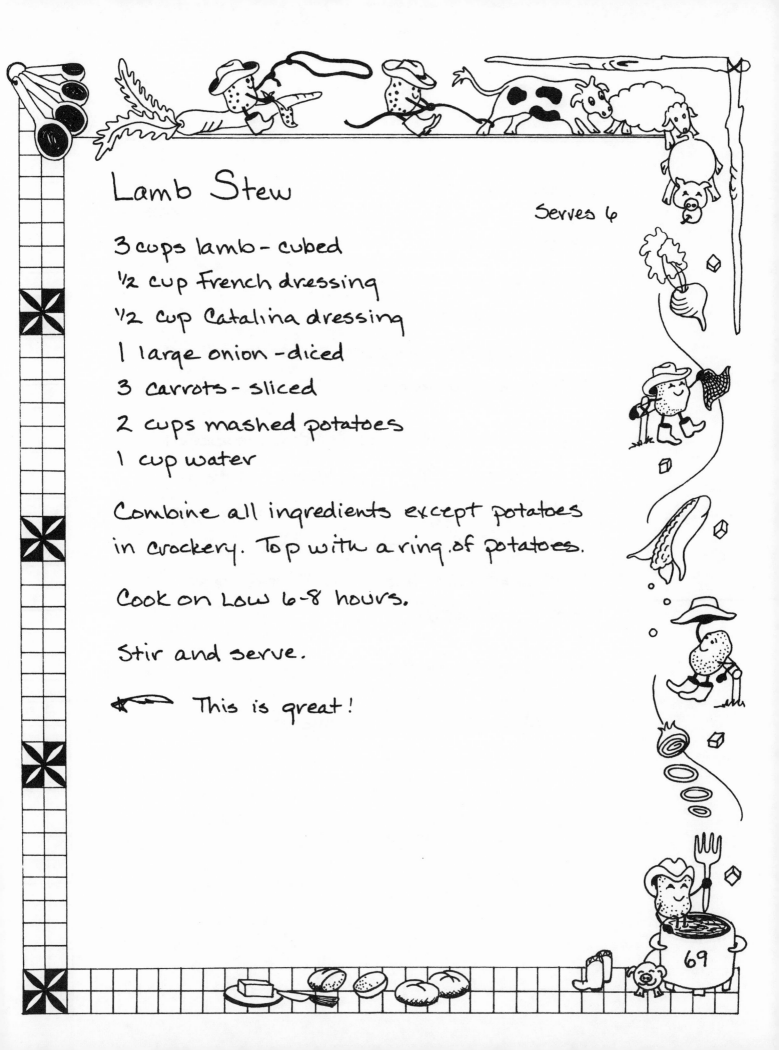

Country Ham

Serves 5

1½ pound ham
¼ cup brown sugar
½ tsp mustard
1 can (16oz) pineapple slices or chunks
2-4 sweet potatoes

Place sweet potatoes in the crockery to form rack. Put the ham on top of the potatoes. In a bowl mix sugar, mustard and a little pineapple juice. Pour over ham along with the rest of the pineapple.

Cook on Low 6-8 hours.

Nice to come home to.

Honey - Orange Glazed Ham

Serves 6

1½ pound ham
¼ cup honey
¼ cup orange juice concentrate
3-4 carrots

Place carrots in the bottom to form a rack. Mix orange juice and honey together and pour over ham on carrots.

Cook on Low 6-8 hours.

★ You can throw in a sweet potato or 2, but this really makes great carrots.

★ Or try pouring 1 cup maple syrup over a ham on a rack of onions.

★ Don't make your rack too high or the meat can't absorb the juices.

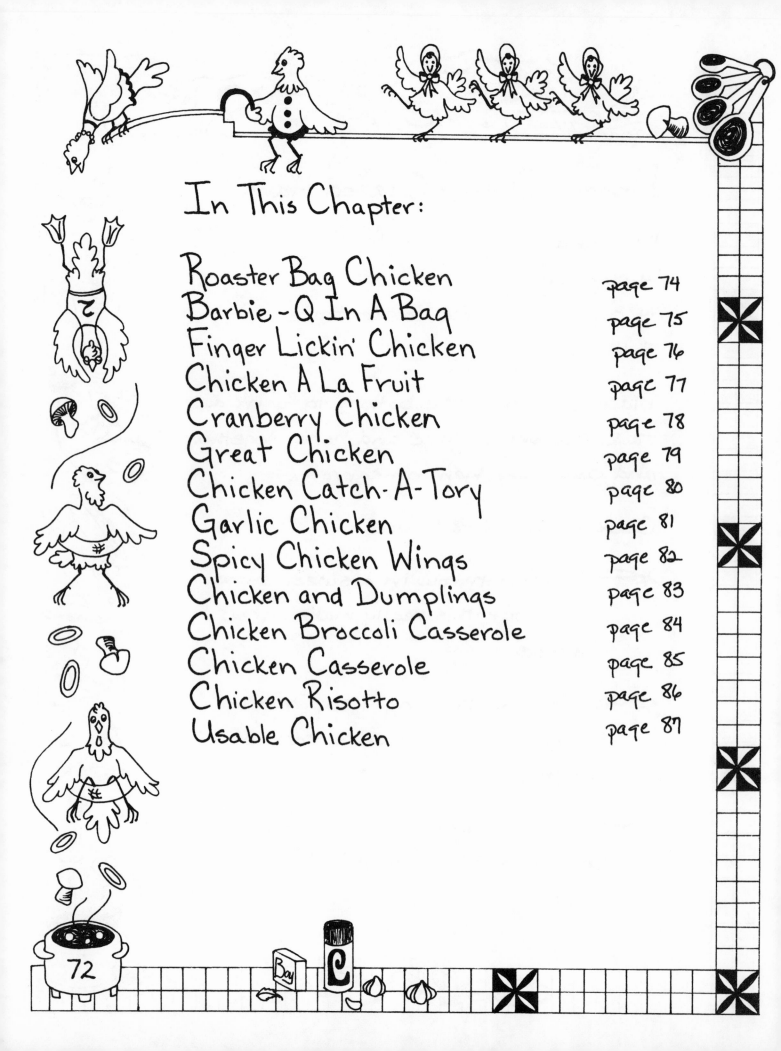

In This Chapter:

Roaster Bag Chicken .... page 74
Barbie-Q In A Bag .... page 75
Finger Lickin' Chicken .... page 76
Chicken A La Fruit .... page 77
Cranberry Chicken .... page 78
Great Chicken .... page 79
Chicken Catch-A-Tory .... page 80
Garlic Chicken .... page 81
Spicy Chicken Wings .... page 82
Chicken and Dumplings .... page 83
Chicken Broccoli Casserole .... page 84
Chicken Casserole .... page 85
Chicken Risotto .... page 86
Usable Chicken .... page 87

Roaster Bag Chicken

Serves 6

1 whole chicken - cut-up

1 envelope onion-mushroom soup mix

1 cup brown rice

1 cup water

1 can cream of chicken soup

Spray crockery with non-stick cooking spray.

Combine rice, water and cream of chicken soup and pour into crockery. Put chicken into a roaster bag with dry soup mix. Inflate the bag, twisting the top and shake to coat the chicken. Puncture 4-6 holes in the bottom of the bag. Fold the top and place the bag on top of the rice.

Cook on Low 8-10 hours.

To serve - place the chicken on a platter and the rice in a bowl.

* You can substitute cream of mushroom soup for the cream of chicken soup.

Barbie-Q In A Bag

Serves 6

1 cup brown rice

1 cup water

1 can cream of mushroom soup

12 chicken thighs

1 envelope B-B-Que flavored Shake-n-Bake

Spray crockery with non-stick cooking spray.

Mix rice, water and soup. Pour it into the crockery. Put the chicken and Shake-n-Bake into a roasting bag. Inflate the bag, twisting the top to trap air and shake to coat the chicken. Poke 3-4 holes in the top of the bag and place on the rice.

Cook on Low 8-10 hours

✱ Kids really like this one.

75

Finger Lickin Chicken

Serves 6

1 whole chicken or pkg of your favorite parts
  in serving size pieces
1 large onion - diced
3/4 pound fresh mushrooms - sliced
1 can cream of mushroom soup
1/2 cup apple juice

Spray your crockery with non-stick spray. Sauté mushrooms and onions in margarine or chicken broth until tender. Mix soup and juice together in a bowl. Dip chicken in the soup mix and pour it in the pot. Top entire mixture with the mushrooms and onions.

Cook on Low 6-8 hours.

Serve with rice or dressing.

Mmm.......

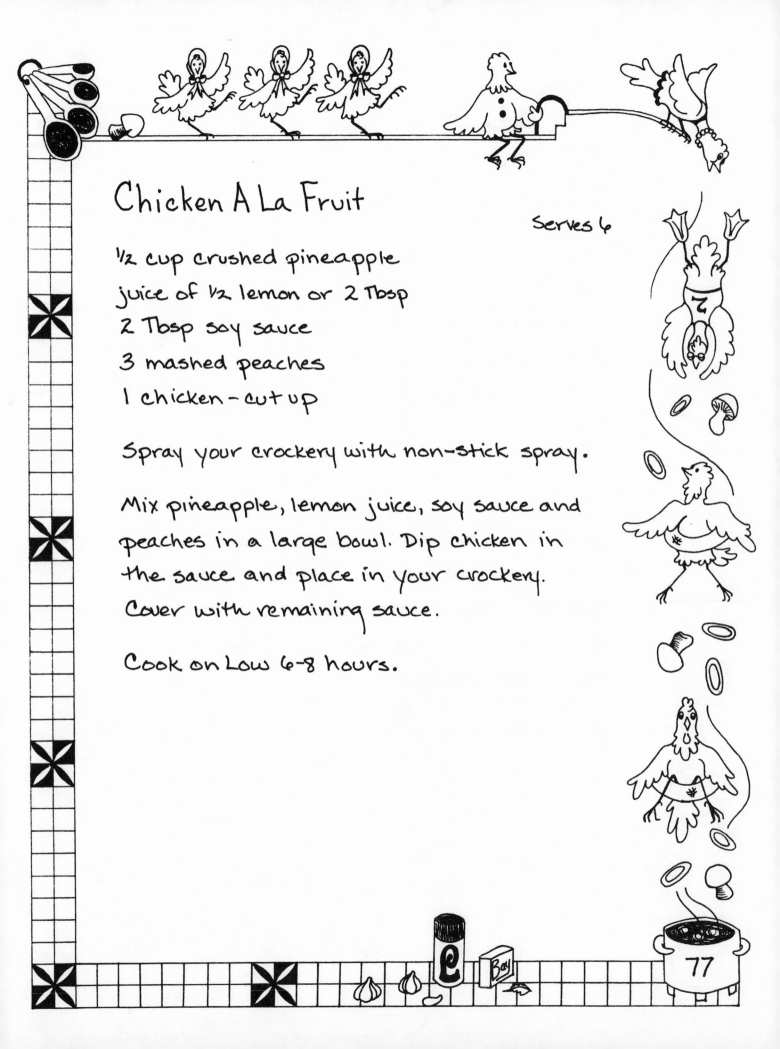

Chicken A La Fruit

Serves 6

½ cup crushed pineapple
juice of ½ lemon or 2 Tbsp
2 Tbsp soy sauce
3 mashed peaches
1 chicken - cut up

Spray your crockery with non-stick spray.

Mix pineapple, lemon juice, soy sauce and peaches in a large bowl. Dip chicken in the sauce and place in your crockery. Cover with remaining sauce.

Cook on Low 6-8 hours.

Cranberry Chicken

Serves 6

1 can whole berry cranberry sauce

1 cup French dressing

1 whole chicken or favorite parts - cut up

3 carrots

1 onion - cut in half

Spray crockery with non-stick cooking spray.

Combine cranberry sauce and French dressing in a bowl. Place onion and carrots in the bottom of crockery as a rack. Dip chicken in sauce and then place on vegetables. Pour remaining sauce over chicken.

Cook on Low 6-8 hours.

Great Chicken

Serves 6

½ cup tomato juice
½ cup soy sauce
½ cup brown sugar
½ cup salad oil
3 garlic cloves - minced
1 whole chicken or favorite parts in serving
    size pieces

Combine all ingredients, except chicken,
in a bowl. Dip each piece of chicken in
the sauce. Place in the crockery. Pour
remaining sauce over the top.

Cook on Low 6-8 hours
        High 3-4 hours

This makes a great marinade for
flank steak. Marinate 2 hours (overnight ok)
and Bar-B-Que.

Thanks, Auntie Jan

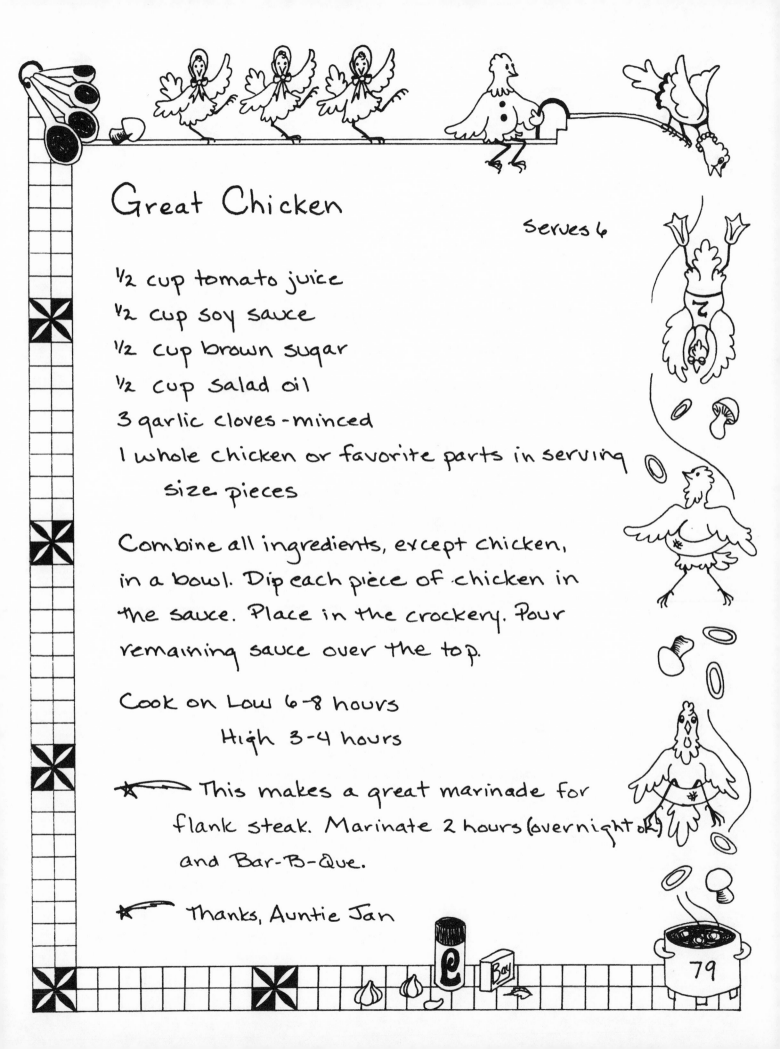

Chicken Catch-A-Tory
"Cacciatore"

Serves 10

1 whole chicken or package of legs and thighs

2 green peppers cut up in large pieces

1 large onion cut up in large pieces

1 pound Italian sausage cut up in 1-2 inch pieces

32 oz spaghetti sauce

1/4 cup water for thick varieties of spaghetti sauce

8 oz mushrooms - cut in half

Combine all ingredients in your crockery.

Cook on Low 8 hours.

Serve over / with spaghetti

* To decrease fat, you can omit sausage or microwave it first.

* Thanks, LuAnne

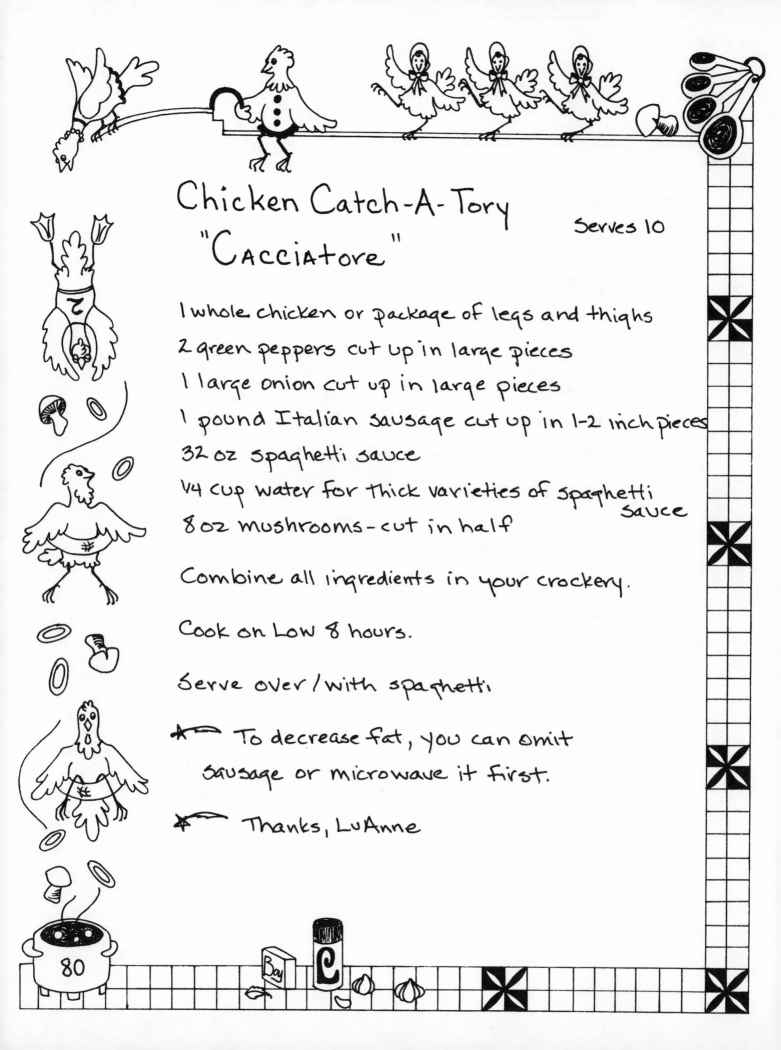

Garlic Chicken or
"It Couldn't Be Easier" Chicken

1 bottle creamy garlic dressing

3 cloves garlic – minced

1 whole chicken or cut-up pieces

Spray crockery with non-stick cooking spray.

Combine ingredients in the crockery.

Cook on Low 8-10 hours,
     High 4 hours.

Spicy Chicken Wings

Serves 4

12 chicken wings

½ cup soy sauce

2 tsp 5 fragrance

1 tsp ginger

2 garlic cloves - minced

2 green onions - chopped

1 tsp or less honey or sugar which you
dilute with water to 1 cup

2 tsp oil

Combine ingredients to make sauce.

Dip chicken in sauce and place in crockery.

Pour remaining sauce over chicken.

Cook on Low 6-8 hours.

★ 5 fragrances makes a big difference
in this recipe. It is available at
Oriental stores. It's other name is 5 spices.

★ This can be a beef marinade; omit oil.

★ Thanks, Peggy

82

Chicken Broccoli Casserole

Serves 6

one crockery of Usable Chicken (page 87)
  made the night before or 2 cups bite size pieces
1 bunch of broccoli ~steamed
sauce: 1 cup Milk
        1/3 cup sour cream
        8 oz cream cheese
        4 oz (1 cup) Cheddar cheese
        1/3 cup Parmasan cheese

Spray crockery with non-stick cooking spray.

Heat all the ingredients of the sauce in a pan,
over medium heat, stirring frequently to
blend cream cheese.
Layer: 1/2 broccoli, 1/2 chicken, 1/2 sauce. Repeat.

Cook on Low 6-8 hours.
Stir gently and serve.

✄ Thanks, Tia

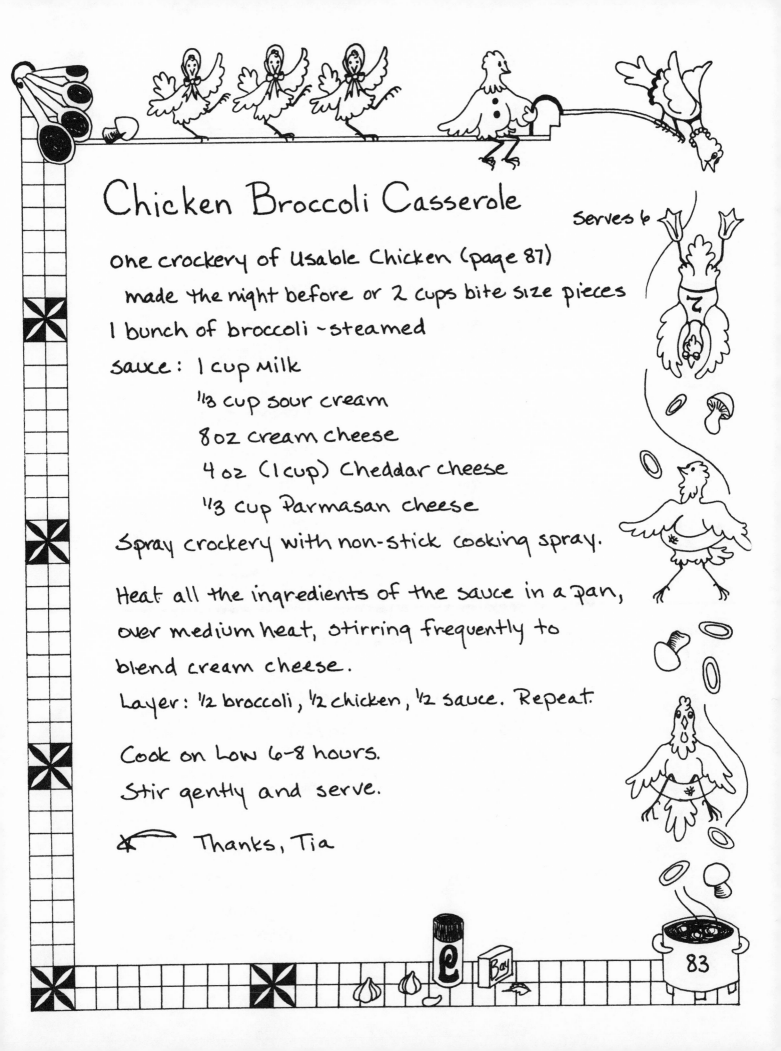

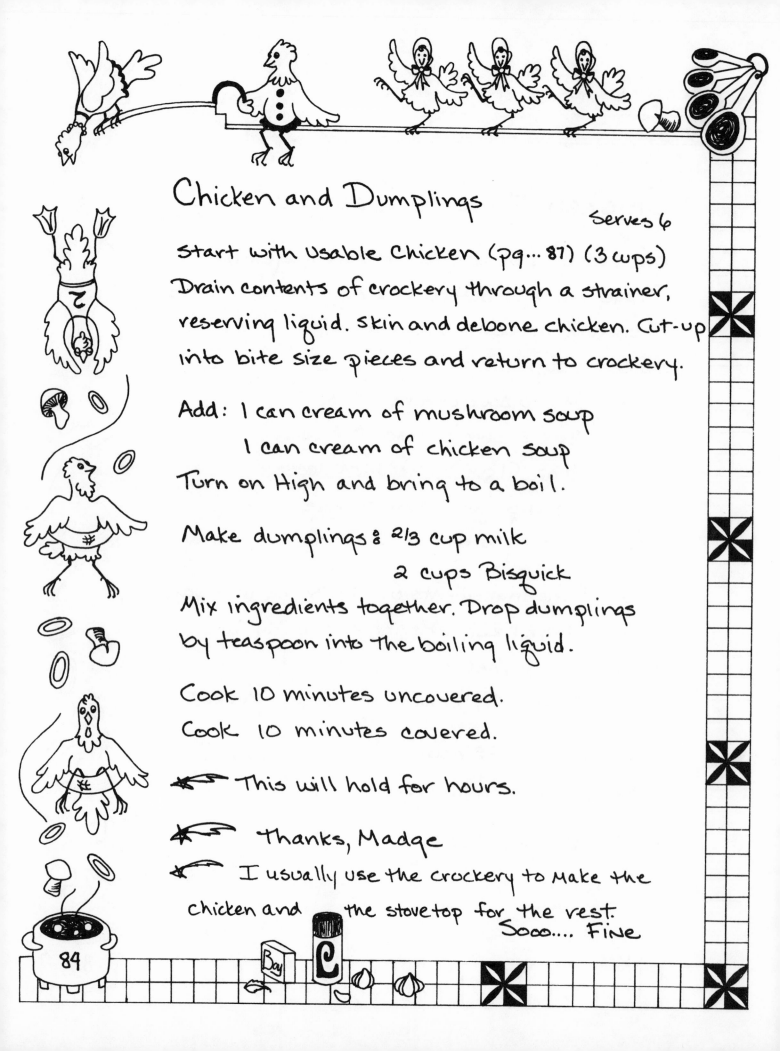

Chicken and Dumplings

Serves 6

Start with usable Chicken (pg...87) (3 cups)
Drain contents of crockery through a strainer,
reserving liquid. Skin and debone chicken. Cut-up
into bite size pieces and return to crockery.

Add: 1 can cream of mushroom soup
     1 can cream of chicken soup
Turn on High and bring to a boil.

Make dumplings: 2/3 cup milk
                2 cups Bisquick
Mix ingredients together. Drop dumplings
by teaspoon into the boiling liquid.

Cook 10 minutes uncovered.
Cook 10 minutes covered.

← This will hold for hours.

← Thanks, Madge

← I usually use the crockery to make the
chicken and the stovetop for the rest.
                                    Sooo.... Fine

84

Chicken Casserole

Serves 6

1 pkg (8oz) dressing (I use Pettridge Farm)

½ stick oleo or butter

1 can cream of mushroom soup

1 can cream of chicken soup

2 cans (15oz) chicken broth or reserved liquid

one crockery of Usable Chicken or

     2 cups Chicken - cut up

Spray crockery with non-stick cooking spray.

Melt butter or oleo and stir into dressing.

In a bowl mix the 2 soups and equal amounts of chicken broth.

Spread a handful of dressing on bottom of crockery.

  Layer: 1 cup chicken, ½ soup, ½ dressing
      Repeat.

Cook on Low 6-8 hours.

★ Great for turkey leftovers

★ Thanks, Mary Sue

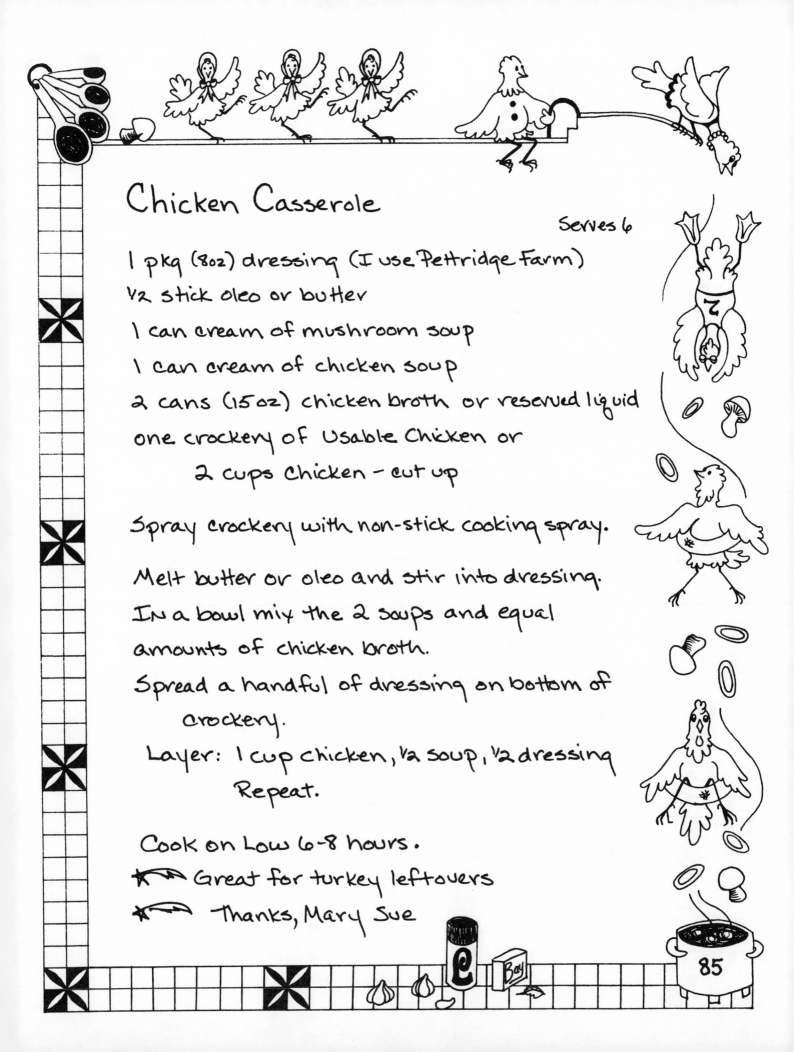

Chicken Risotto

Serves 10

1¼ cups brown rice

1 can cream of mushroom soup

1 can cream of chicken soup

¼ cup melted margarine

¼ cup apple juice

10-12 pieces of chicken

½ cup slivered almonds

⅓ cup grated Parmesan cheese

Spray crockery with non-stick cooking spray.

In a bowl combine soups, margarine and juice. Place rice in crockery and pour ½ soup mixture to cover. Place chicken in next. Pour remaining soup over chicken. Top with almonds and cheese.

Cook on Low 8-10 hours

It's delicious.

Usable Chicken

Serves 6

1 whole chicken or package of your favorite parts

4 cups water

2 Tbsp parsley

2 tsp garlic salt

1-2 bay leaves

1 Tbsp minced onion or onion flakes

1 tsp Lawry's seasoning salt

Place all ingredients in the crockery.

Cook on Low 6-8 hours,
        High 3-4 hours.

☛ Chicken frozen? - No problem. Just cover with warm water.

☛ I usually put this on the night before so the chicken is ready to use for soups, casseroles, or Mexican food.

87

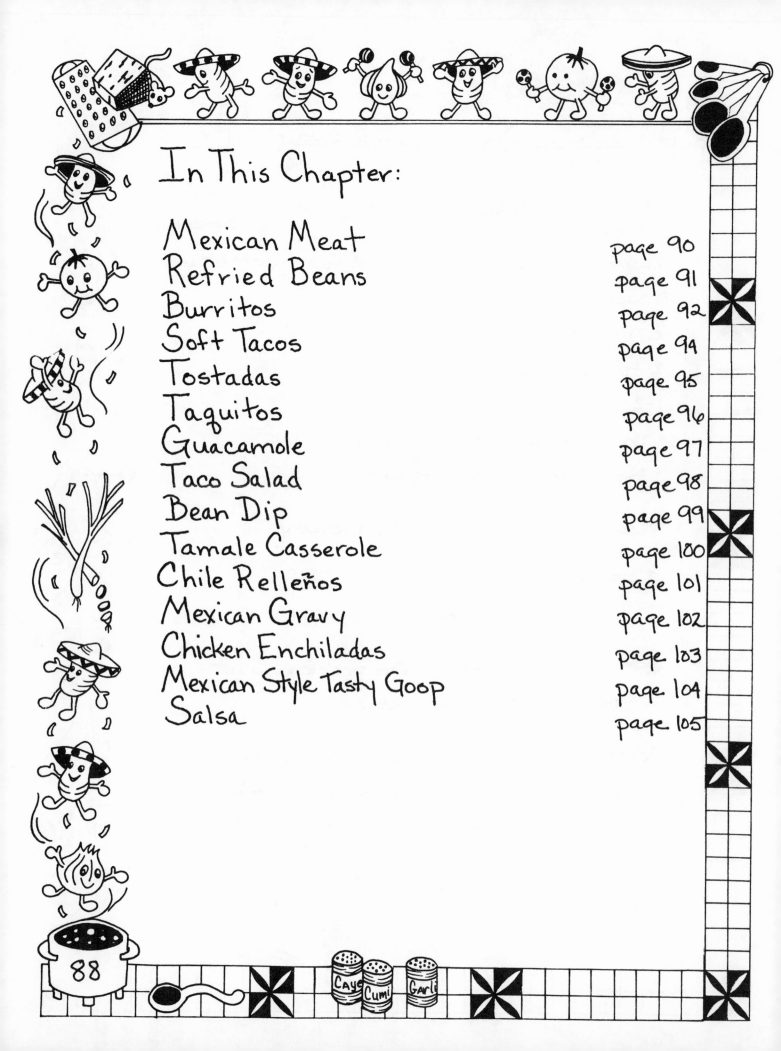

In This Chapter:

Mexican Meat .... page 90
Refried Beans .... page 91
Burritos .... page 92
Soft Tacos .... page 94
Tostadas .... page 95
Taquitos .... page 96
Guacamole .... page 97
Taco Salad .... page 98
Bean Dip .... page 99
Tamale Casserole .... page 100
Chile Relleños .... page 101
Mexican Gravy .... page 102
Chicken Enchiladas .... page 103
Mexican Style Tasty Goop .... page 104
Salsa .... page 105

Mexican Meat

3 pounds stew beef
1 can (10 oz) cream of celery soup
1 can (4 oz) chopped green chiles

Combine all ingredients in crockery
Stir well to coat meat.

Cook on High 6-8 hours.

Use a potato masher to blend liquid
and separate meat. It should just
fall apart when done.

Use this recipe for: Burritos
                     Soft Tacos
                     Tostadas
                     Bean Dip
or some like it just over rice.

★ —— I can make 10-20 burritos, tacos,
         tostadas or taquitos.
★ —— This is the recipe that started
         the book.

                          Enjoy.

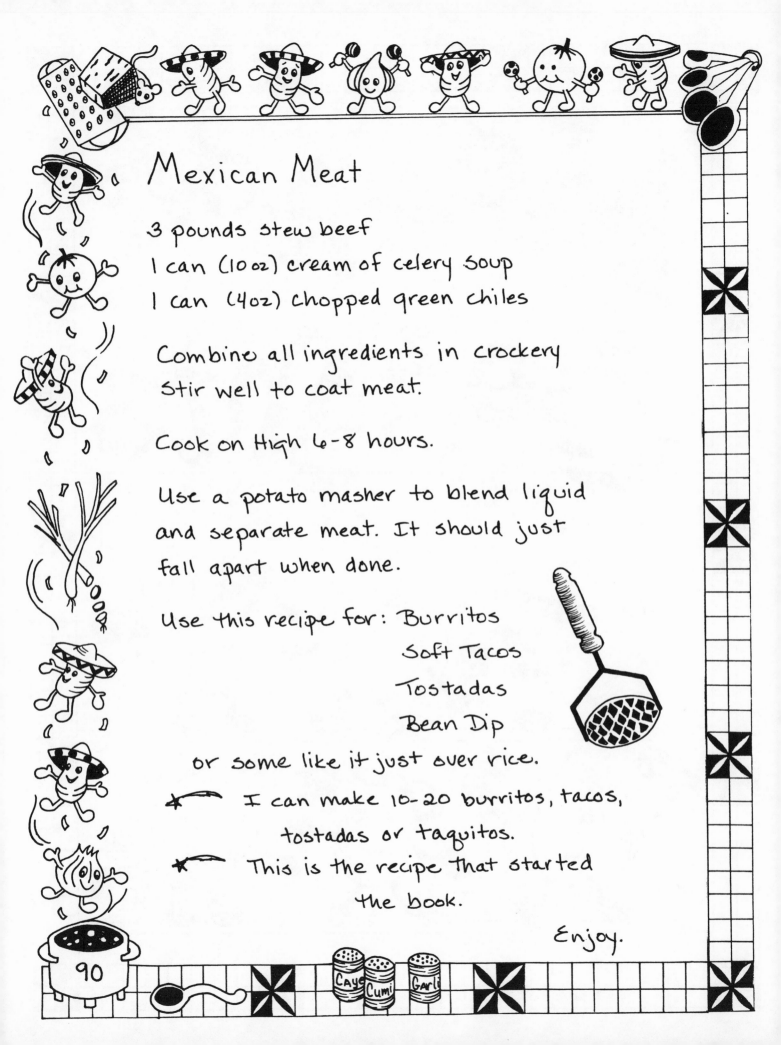

Refried Beans

Serves 10

1 pound (2 cups) dry pinto beans
4 cups water
1 cup coffee (already brewed)
3 cloves garlic - minced
1 large onion - diced
1 Tbsp cumin
2 tsp chili powder
1½ tsp oregano
1 tsp salt

Place all the ingredients in the crockery and stir well.

Cook on Low 8-10 hours

Mash with a potato masher to blend.
You can serve as is or refry the beans in bacon grease. This step is optional.

Use this recipe for: Burritos   Bean Dip
                      Tostadas   Soft Tacos
                      Taco Salad   A side dish

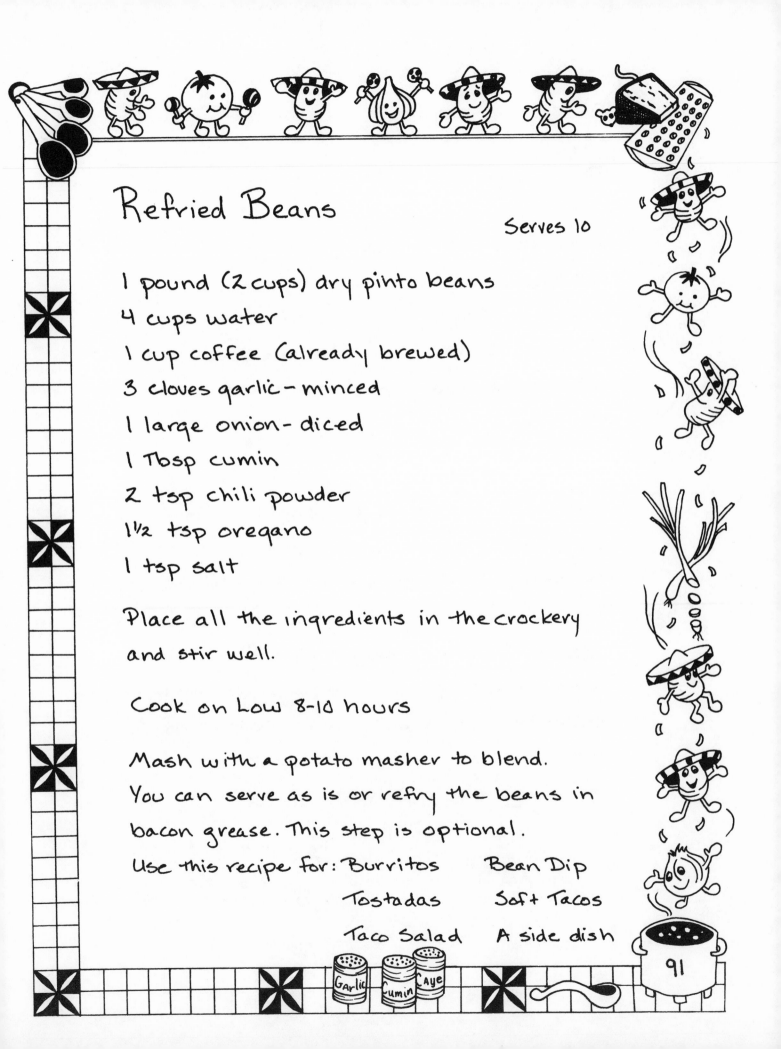

Burritos

Flour tortillas - 1-2 per person

All other ingredients are optional:

Mexican Meat	tomatoes - chopped
Refried Beans	lettuce or sprouts
cheese - grated	hot sauce
onions - diced	sour cream

Line up all desired ingredients for easy assembly. You need to warm the tortilla so it won't crack. I zap it in the microwave for 20-30 seconds. Or you can use a cast iron fry pan that you rub a little oil in; lay it down and flip it over. Then working quickly spread 2 heaping tablespoons of meat in the center of the tortilla. Cover with 1-2 tablespoons of each desired ingredient.

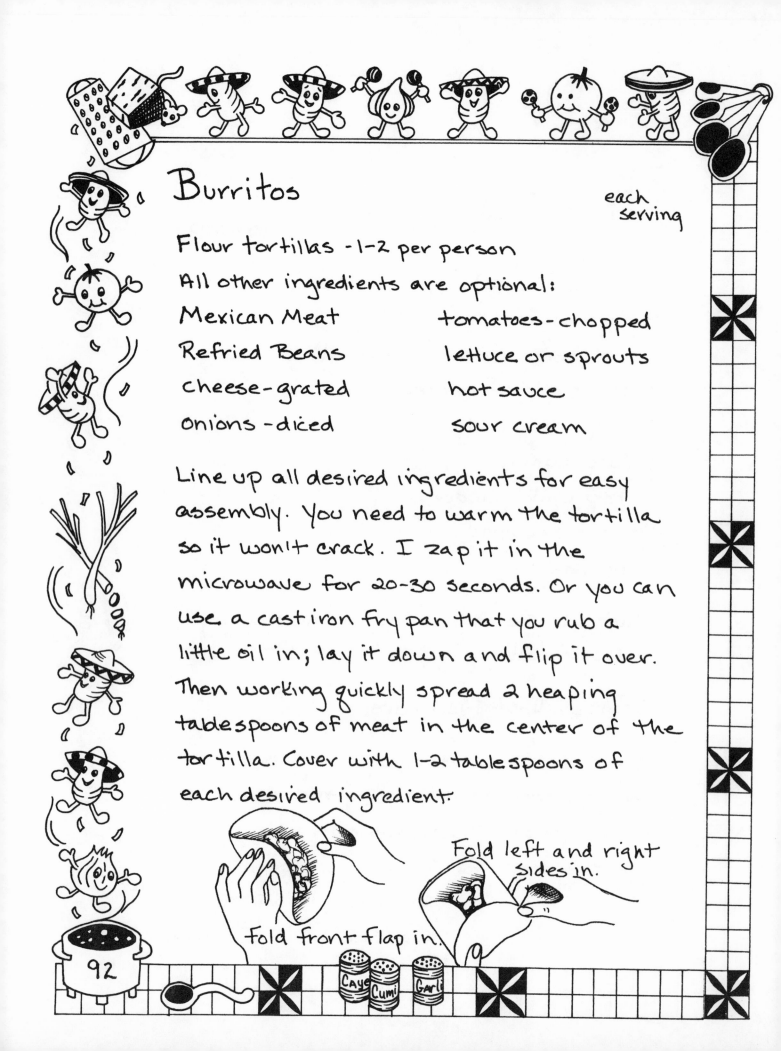

Fold front flap in.

Fold left and right sides in.

92

Roll burrito over - away from you - the weight holds last flap.

Quayle's Favorite

Zap tortilla for 20 seconds. Fill with meat, beans, cheese, sour cream, lettuce, tomatoes, "lotsa" onions, and pour on the hot sauce. Fold and zap 2½ minutes. Top with more hot sauce and serve with a fork.

My Favorite

Place cheese on tortilla and zap for 40 seconds (until cheese melts). Fill with beans, a little meat juice, scant onion, "lotsa" sour cream and a heap of sprouts. Fold with a little pushing to smash sprouts.

The sour cream is hard to spread on the top of a mound - so I spread it on one flap of the tortilla.

Burritos look alike when assembled. I serve on paper plates so I can write the name on the plate (kids love it).

You can fill a tortilla with anything - leftovers can be interesting.

Garlic Cumin Caye

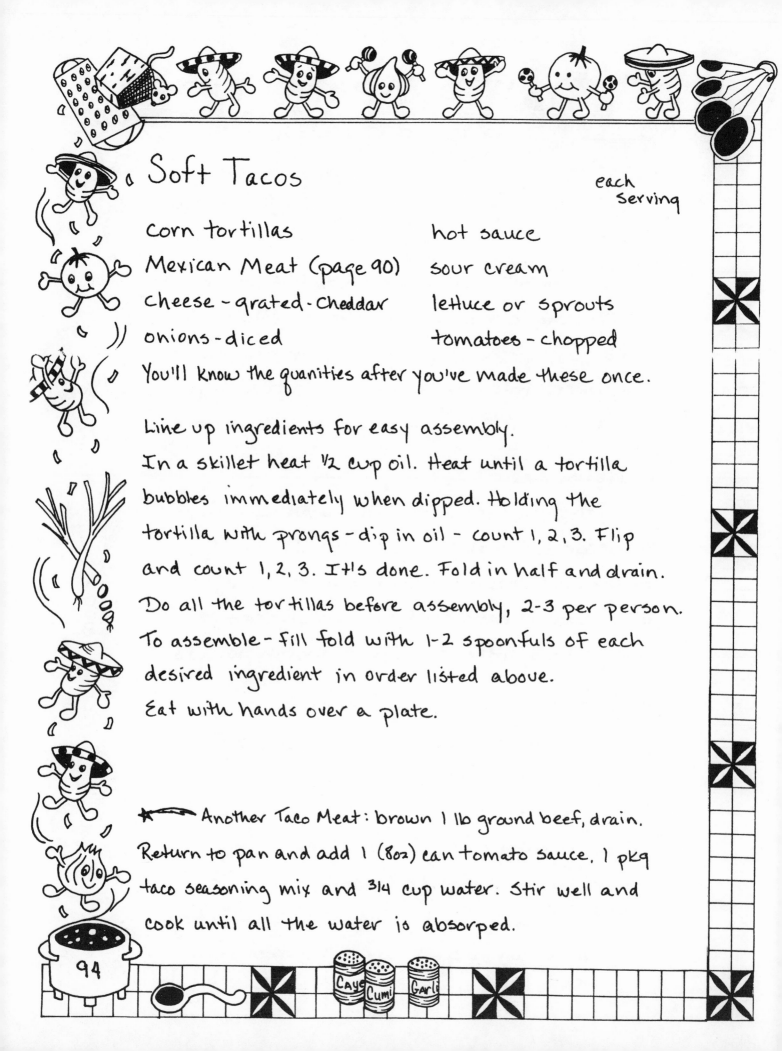

Soft Tacos

Corn tortillas   hot sauce

Mexican Meat (page 90)   sour cream

cheese - grated - Cheddar   lettuce or sprouts

onions - diced   tomatoes - chopped

You'll know the quanities after you've made these once.

Line up ingredients for easy assembly.

In a skillet heat ½ cup oil. Heat until a tortilla bubbles immediately when dipped. Holding the tortilla with prongs - dip in oil - count 1, 2, 3. Flip and count 1, 2, 3. It's done. Fold in half and drain.

Do all the tortillas before assembly, 2-3 per person.

To assemble - fill fold with 1-2 spoonfuls of each desired ingredient in order listed above.

Eat with hands over a plate.

★ Another Taco Meat: brown 1 lb ground beef, drain. Return to pan and add 1 (8oz) can tomato sauce. 1 pkg taco seasoning mix and ¾ cup water. Stir well and cook until all the water is absorped.

Tostadas

corn tortillas	hot sauce
Refried Beans (page 91)	lettuce - chopped
Mexican Meat (page 90)	Guacamole (page 97)
cheese - grated	sour cream
onion - diced	tomatoes

each Serving

Line up ingredients for easy assembly.
In a skillet heat ½ cup oil. Fry a
tortilla until stiff. Remove and drain
on a paper towel.

To assemble - gently spread refried beans
over entire tortilla. Cover with meat, cheese,
onions, and hot sauce. Build a mound of
lettuce and top with sour cream, guacamole,
and tomatoes. Pick up and eat with hands
or use utensils.

sour cream ←
onions ←
meat ←
tortilla ←

→ tomatoes
→ lettuce
→ cheese
→ refried beans

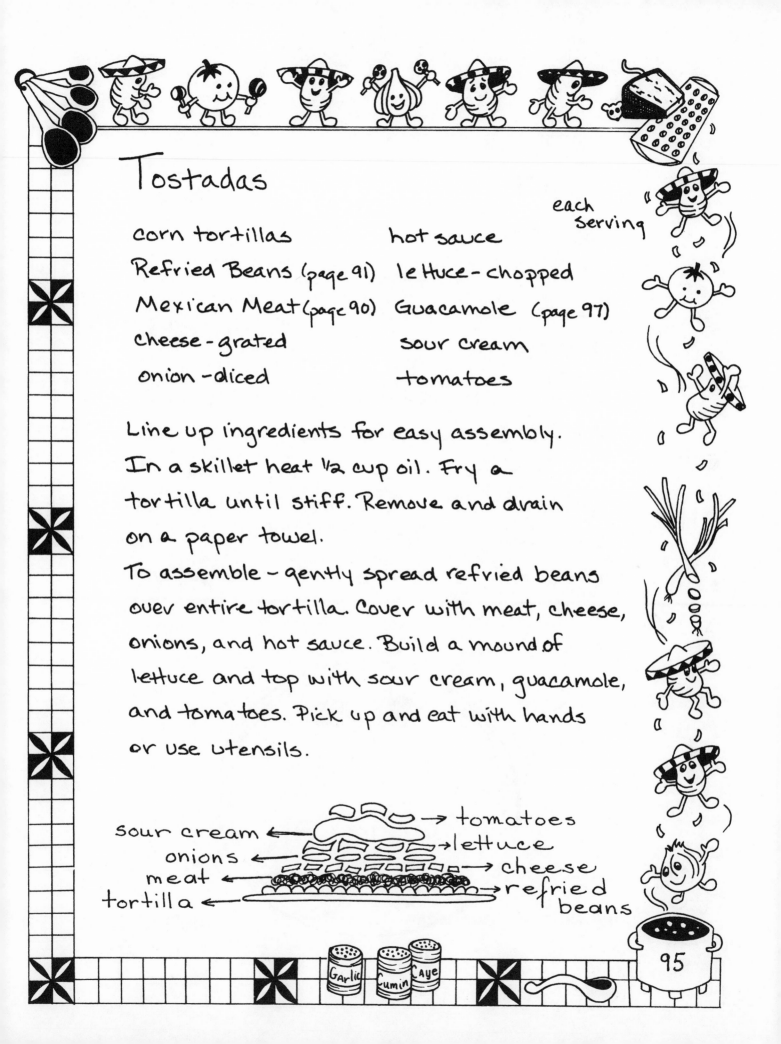

95

Taquitos

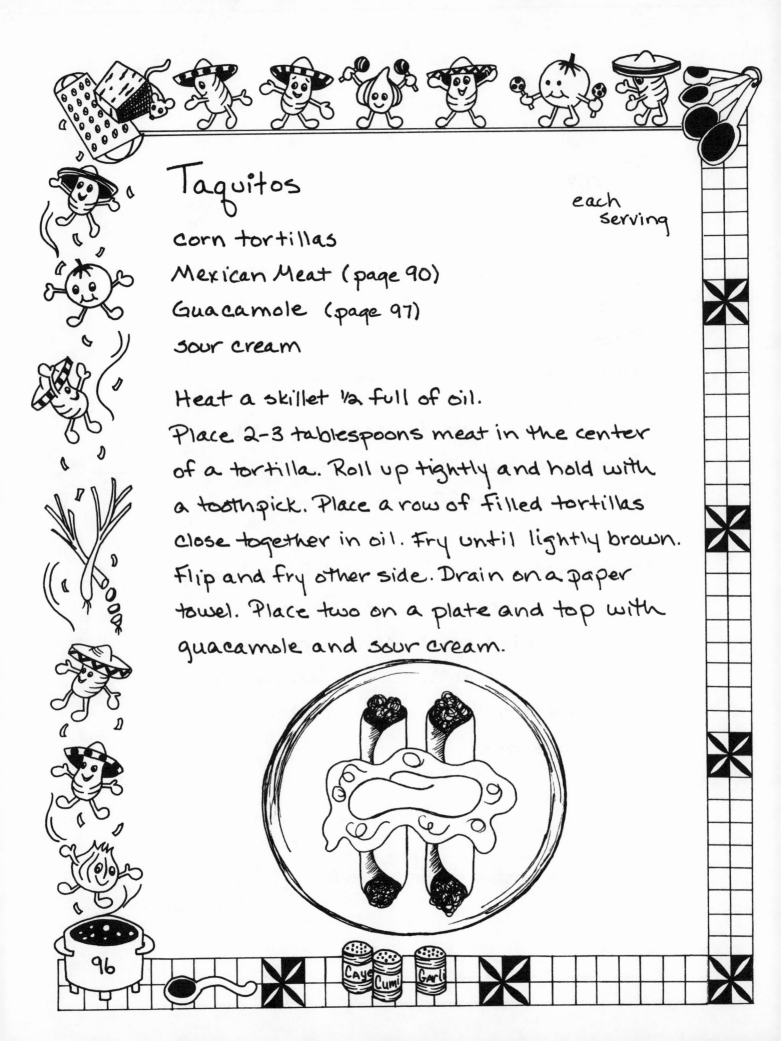

each serving

corn tortillas

Mexican Meat (page 90)

Guacamole (page 97)

sour cream

Heat a skillet ½ full of oil.
Place 2-3 tablespoons meat in the center
of a tortilla. Roll up tightly and hold with
a toothpick. Place a row of filled tortillas
close together in oil. Fry until lightly brown.
Flip and fry other side. Drain on a paper
towel. Place two on a plate and top with
guacamole and sour cream.

96

Guacamole

Makes a bowl full

3 avacados

juice of a ½ a lemon

1-2 Tbsp finely chopped onion

1 Tbsp salsa or taco sauce

½ tsp garlic powder

½ tsp Lawry's seasoning salt

2 Tbsp mayonaise

1 tomato finely chopped

Peel, pit and mash avacados. Squeeze
the ½ lemon over top and stir. Add rest
of ingredients and mix well. Taste.
Adjust seasonings to personal liking.
Use this recipe for: Taquitos
                    Tostadas
Or even try in or on: Tacos
                    Taco Salad
                    chips

Taco Salad

Serves 8

3 medium avacados

2 Tbsp lemon juice

½ tsp salt

1 cup sour cream

½ cup mayonaise

1 package taco seasoning

2 cups Refried Beans (page 91)

1 bunch green onions - chopped

3 medium tomatoes - chopped

2 (3½ oz) cans chopped olives

8 oz cheddar cheese

Tortilla chips

Peel, pit and mash avacados. Mix in lemon and salt. Set aside. In a bowl, mix sour cream, mayo and taco seasoning.

To assemble - spread refried beans to cover a large platter. Top with avacado mixture. Spread with sour cream mixture. Sprinkle onions, tomatoes and olives. Top with cheese. Chill or serve as is with chips.

Bean Dip

Serves 8

2 cups Refried Beans (page 91)

1 cup Mexican Meat (page 90)

1 pound process American cheese - cubed

2 Tbsp taco sauce

1 Tbsp taco spice

1 tsp garlic salt

Combine all ingredients in the crockery.

Cook on High 45 minutes (until cheese melts), then keep on Low (up to 6 hours).

Serve with chips.

Yummy

Tamale Casserole

Serves 10

1 pound ground pork

½ pound ground beef

1 large onion - chopped

⅓ cup oil

28 oz can whole tomatoes

1 cup corn meal

1 can whole kernel corn

2 eggs

1 tsp garlic salt

1 Tbsp chili powder

Spray crockery with non-stick cooking spray.

Brown pork and beef, drain and set aside.
Sauté onions in oil. Puree tomatoes in blender.
When onions are slightly brown, add tomatoes.
Stirring well, add corn meal very, very
slowly. Stir constantly to prevent lumping.
Add meat and corn. Beat eggs lightly and
add with spices. Pour into crockery.
Cook on Low 6-8 hours.

☞ You can substitute Mexican Meat for beef and pork

Chile Relleños

Serves 8

2 cans (4oz each) whole green chiles

½ pound Monterey Jack cheese -grated

½ pound Cheddar cheese - grated

2 Tbsp flour

2 eggs

1 can evaporated milk (12 oz)

1 can (8oz) tomato sauce

Open chiles and remove seeds and veins.

In a bowl combine flour, eggs and milk.

Spray crockery with non- stick cooking spray.

In bottom of crockery layer: ½ chiles,

½ of each cheese and pour ½ milk mix.

Repeat.

Cook on Low 6-8 hours.

Last ½ hour (or whenever top looks

solid) pour tomato sauce on top.

← This dish lasts well in the crockery.

← Thanks, Tom

Mexican Gravy

½ stick butter

1½ cup chili powder

⅓ cup flour

½ tsp garlic salt

¼ tsp cumin

¼ tsp oregano

3 cans (15oz) chicken broth

1 can (12oz) tomato sauce

Melt butter in a pan. In a bowl, mix together dry ingredients. Slowly add dry ingredients to butter, stirring slowly and constantly. It will become crumbly. Very slowly, add chicken broth. Add tomato sauce and you should have a thick, tasty sauce.

I pour this into a slow cooker to blend and keep warm, but my sister uses it immediately.

One batch makes a dozen enchiladas.

★ The chili powder is the correct amount. Try it, you'll like it.

★ Thanks, Betty.

Chicken Enchiladas

Serves 12

One crockery of Usable Chicken (made night before)
(about 3 cups)

1 can (4oz) chopped green chiles

1 onion - diced

1 batch Mexican Gravy

4oz each, Monterey Jack, and Cheddar cheese - grated

1 can chopped olives

1 dozen corn tortillas

Filling: skin, debone and cut up chicken. Stir in chiles, onion, and one cup gravy.

Assembly: dip tortilla in gravy and lie flat. Fill center with 3 Tbsp filling and roll tightly. Place seam side down in a 9x13 pan. Pour any extra sauce over top. Cover with cheese. Top with olives.

Bake 350° x 30 minutes. Serve with sour cream.

Variation: Fill dipped tortilla with a handful of cheese, roll and top with more. Bake as above or Microwave (my favorite).

These can be baked in your crockery but it's more like a casserole.

I love you, Jan

103

Mexican-Style Tasty Goop

Serves 10

one crockery of Usable Chicken (made night before)
   or 2-3 cups chicken -diced   page...

1 onion -diced

2 cans cream of mushroom soup

1/2 cube margarine (1/8 lb)

2 cans (4oz each) chopped green chiles

1 chicken flavored bouillon cube

1 cup hot water

6 oz Cheddar cheese - grated

1 pkg (a dozen) CORN tortillas - cut up into
   bite size pieces

Spray crockery with non-stick cooking spray

Sauté onions in margarine until soft. Add
chicken, chiles, bouillon, water and soup.

Layer: 1/2 tortillas, 1/2 chicken mix, 1/2 cheese
   Repeat.

Cook on Low 6-8 hours.

Stir well and serve with sour cream.

Caye Cumi Garli

Salsa

4 large tomatoes - skinned and seeded
1 can (4oz) chopped green chiles
3 green onions - chopped
1 Tbsp vinegar
1 tsp garlic salt

Chop tomatoes and mix with the rest
of the ingredients. Chill 2-3 hours.

★⟶ I know this isn't a crockery recipe
but you have all the rest of my
favorites - thought I'd complete the
chapter with this one.

★⟶ Serve with chips or use
in burritos, tacos, tostadas,
guacamole, bean dip, or enchiladas.

★⟶ You can substitute canned tomatoes,
28 oz, but you need to remove core and
seeds.

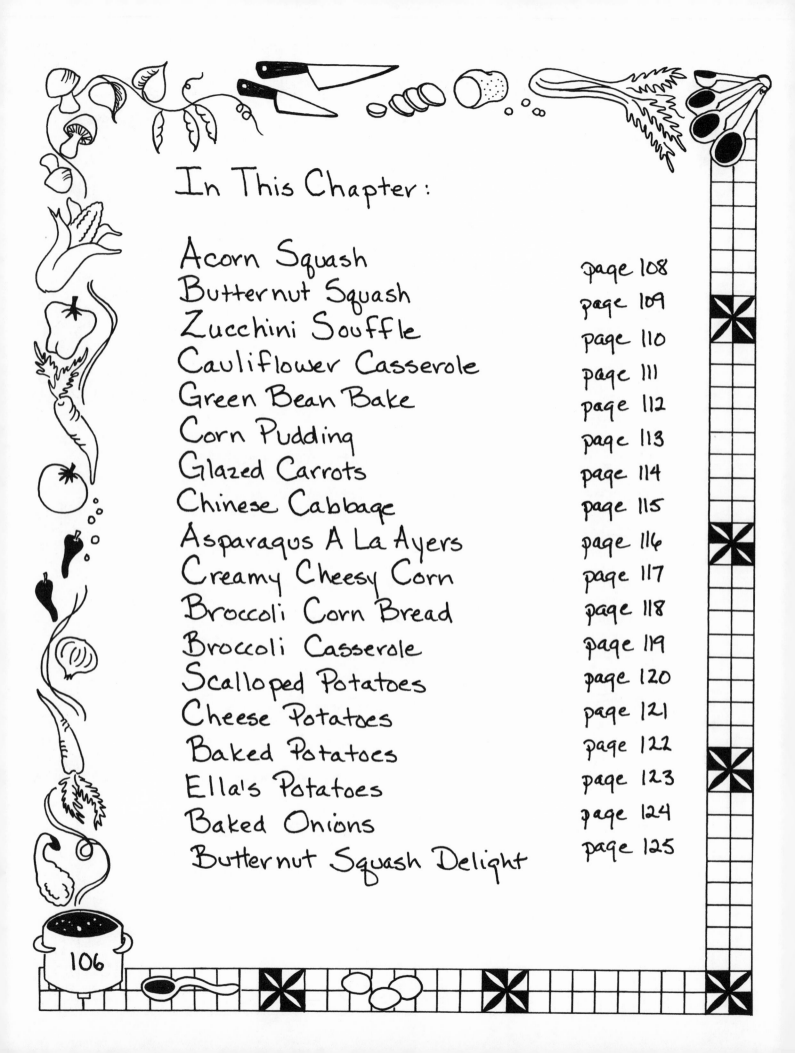

In This Chapter:

Acorn Squash .... page 108
Butternut Squash .... page 109
Zucchini Souffle .... page 110
Cauliflower Casserole .... page 111
Green Bean Bake .... page 112
Corn Pudding .... page 113
Glazed Carrots .... page 114
Chinese Cabbage .... page 115
Asparagus A La Ayers .... page 116
Creamy Cheesy Corn .... page 117
Broccoli Corn Bread .... page 118
Broccoli Casserole .... page 119
Scalloped Potatoes .... page 120
Cheese Potatoes .... page 121
Baked Potatoes .... page 122
Ella's Potatoes .... page 123
Baked Onions .... page 124
Butternut Squash Delight .... page 125

Acorn Squash

Serves 4

1 acorn squash
1/3 cup water

Scrub squash and place in crockery with water.

Cook on Low 6-8 hours.

Remove with a mitt or towel. Cut in half, scrap out seeds and then scrape squash into a bowl. Season with butter and allspice or cinnamon or nutmeg.

➤ This is so easy and so good. Squash is a wonderful food, but seems like it takes along time to cook - or rather wait for.

➤ Or try it like butternut squash recipe.

Butternut Squash

Serves 4

1 butternut squash   cinnamon
¼ cup water   margarine

Cut the squash in half and scrape out
the seeds. Sprinkle with cinnamon and
a pat of margarine. Wrap in foil. Place
in crockery.

Cook on Low 6-8 hours.

★ ➔ Red hots are fun to season
     with in the fall.

★ ➔ Most squash will adapt to the
     cooking method on these two pages.

★ ➔ Thanks, Linda for _all_ your help.
     Your comments, corrections and laughter
     were very encouraging.

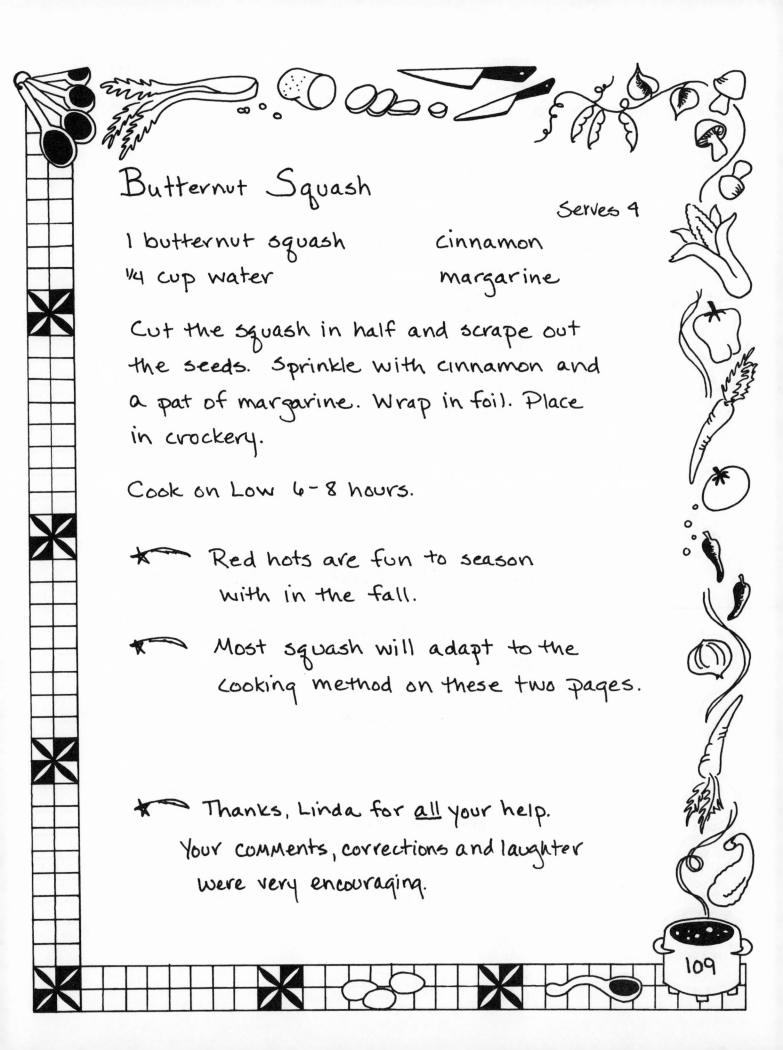

Zucchini Souffle

Serves 6

4 cups grated zucchini

1¾ cup Bisquick

¾ cup Parmasan cheese

¼ cup oil

4 eggs beaten

1 large onion - diced

3 garlic cloves - minced

3 Tbsp parsley

salt to taste

Spray crockery with non-stick cooking spray.

Combine all ingredients in a bowl. Pour into crockery.

Cook on Low 6-8 hours

Thanks, Rosie and congratulations on Joe, Jr.

110

Cauliflower Casserole

Serves 10

3 cups cooked rice

1 head cauliflower - cut into flowerettes - slice stems

1 can cream of mushroom soup

½ pound mushrooms - sliced

2 cups grated cheese (cheddar or Monterey Jack)

½ cup water

1 medium onion - diced

Spray crockery with non-stick cooking spray.

Combine all ingredients. Mixture will be chunky but stir well.

Cook on Low 4-6 hours.

★ The cauliflower holds up well but the color is dull. You can add peas for color, if you like.

★ Ever used an egg slicer for mushrooms?

Green Bean Bake

Serves 6

2 pkg frozen green beans
1 can cream of mushroom soup
⅓ cup milk
1 tsp soy sauce
1 small can French fried onions

Spray crockery with non-stick cooking spray.

Boil green beans until separated and defrosted (about 3 minutes). In a bowl mix soup, milk and soy until smooth. Add beans and ½ of the onions. Pour it into the crockery. Top with remaining onions.

Cook on Low 4-6 hours.

↞ This is not good with canned beans.

↞ the top onions don't get crunchies like when baked, but I love this recipe for pot luck take-alongs.

Corn Pudding

Serves 8

1 can cream style corn (1 lb 1oz)

1 can whole kernel corn (1 lb 1oz)

8 oz sour cream

1 stick margarine - melted

2 eggs - beaten

1 box Jiffy corn meal mix

Spray crockery with non-stick cooking spray.

Combine all ingredients in a large bowl.
Pour into the crockery.

Cook on Low 6-8 hours.

← You can cook it on High 4 hours, but it gives you a brown, crisp ring around the outside.

← Thanks, Donny and Richard

Glazed Carrots

Serves 6

¼ cup butter or margarine

2 tsp cornstarch

⅓ cup honey

1 tsp lemon juice

⅛ tsp cinnamon

3 cups carrots - sliced

Melt butter, blend in cornstarch. Add honey, lemon and cinnamon. Stir well. When mixture starts to boil, stir in carrots. Pour into crockery.

Cook on Low 6-8 hours.

For a summer dish - stir in 1 cup halved grapes before serving.

Chinese Cabbage

Serves 6

1 head of Chinese cabbage
1 large can V-8 juice

Remove the stalk base, cutting the cabbage to fit in the crockery. Pour juice to cover.

Cook on Low 6-10 hours,
        High 3-6 hours.

✰   I don't know why I love this so much. Maybe be cause it helped me loose weight. I love to eat it with chopsticks and a bowl of brown rice.

✰   This is an ugly looking recipe, but try it anyway.

Asparagus A La Ayers

Serves 6

1 can (15oz) asparagus tips
1 pkg (12 oz) frozen peas
1 can (8oz) sliced water chestnuts
1 can (10oz) cream of mushroom soup
½ pound Cheddar cheese - grated

Spray your crockery with non-stick cooking spray.

Combine all the ingredients and pour into the crockery.

Cook on High 2-3 hours.
        Low 4-6 hours.

   I like to take this to eat togethers
and let people guess the contents.

Creamy Cheesy Corn

Serves 6

1 can (15oz) cream style corn

2 cans (15oz each) whole kernel corn

8 oz cream cheese

Combine all the ingredients in the crockery.

Cook on Low 4-6 hours.

        High 2½-3 hours.

← This doubles nicely for a political pot luck.

← Thanks, Donna

Broccoli Corn Bread

Serves 8

1 stick (¼ lb) margarine - melted

1 pkg (10oz) chopped broccoli - cooked and drained

1 onion - chopped

1 box corn bread mix

4 eggs well beaten

8 oz cottage cheese

1 tsp salt

Spray crockery with non-stick cooking spray.

Combine all ingredients. Stir well and pour into crockery.

Cook on Low 6-8 hours.

You can serve like spoon bread or cut around it with a knife, invert pot and it should remove easily. Cut in wedges.

I was given this recipe at a picnic for deaf interpeters. Thank you, kind lady, for your patience with my sign language skills.

Broccoli Casserole

2 pkg frozen broccoli

1 can cream of mushroom soup

½ pound mushrooms - sliced

3/4 cup cheddar cheese - grated

3/4 cup mayonaise

½ cup grated cheddar cheese

3/4 cup crushed crackers

Cook broccoli and combine with next 4 ingredients. Pour into your crockery.

Cook on Low 4-6 hours.

Top with the second portion of cheese and crackers the last hour.

Scalloped Potatoes

Serves 8

5-6 potatoes - peeled and sliced

1 onion - diced   grated cheese for garnish

¼ cup flour

1 tsp salt

2 Tbsp butter

1 can (10oz) cream of mushroom soup

Spray crockery with non-stick cooking spray.

Mix melted butter and soup together - set aside.

Layer: ½ potatoes

   ½ onion

      ½ flour and salt

Repeat layers.

Pour soup over top.

Cook on Low 8-10 hours,

   High 3-4 hours.

Serve garnished with grated cheese.

🠐 Cubed ham goes well in this.

120

Cheese Potatoes

Serves 8

4 large potatoes

1 cup sour cream

1 onion -diced

1 tsp salt

1 pound cheese -grated (your favorite kind)

salt and pepper to taste

1 Tbsp butter or margarine

Boil potatoes, cool and grate. Combine all ingredients and plop it in the crockery. Dot the top with butter and sprinkle on a little paprika.

Cook on Low 4-6 hours.

Try cooking the potatoes in your crockery the night before.

Thanks, Pat

Baked Potatoes

each

1 potato per person

Scrub potatoes and place in crockery on top of a rack.

Form a rack by:
1) layer of carrots
2) aluminum foil crushed up
3) two coat hangers bent in a U shape
4) or just wrap potatoes in foil

Cook on Low 8-10 hours
          High 4-5 hours

* Skins turn out soft, especially in foil.

* You can make mashed potatoes too. If you don't peel the potatoes they turn out darker with a slightly different taste. If you do peel, I suggest you do it before cooking.

* Thanks, Tato.

Ella's Potatoes

Serves 10

The night before: place in crockery

    8-10 potatoes - scrubbed

Cook on Low overnight (6-10 hours).

In the morning:

    Peel and mash potatoes

Combine:

    potatoes

    ½ cup margarine

    1 tsp salt

    1 tsp Lawry's seasoning salt

    1 cup scalded milk

    8 oz cream cheese

You can stir or whip with a mixer.

Spray crockery with non-stick cooking spray.

Place potato mixture into crockery.

Cook on Low 6-8 hours.

✱ Actually, I like to use this recipe
   for leftover baked potatoes.

Baked Onions

Serves 6

6-8 onions

Place onions in your crockery – skin and all

Cook on Low 6-8 hours

Remove from crockery and cut top and bottom off (I hold it with a paper towel). Squeeze the onion and the delicious part will pop out – leaving the skin to be discarded. Top with salt and margarine.

You can Bar-B-Que onions in the same way. Just place on the fire with skins and when black and starting to bubble (soft), remove, cut, pop out and coat with butter and salt.

A real treat...

Is your crockery plugged in?

Is it turned on?

Butternut Squash Delight

Serves 8

3 cups cooked and mashed squash

½ cup sugar or ¼ cup honey

dash salt

¼ cup evaporated milk

¼ cup butter or margarine

2 eggs slightly beaten

1 tsp vanilla

½ cup coconut

½ cup walnuts

½ cup brown sugar

½ stick butter or margarine (4 Tbsp)

¼ cup flour

Spray your crockery with non-stick spray.

Combine the first 8 ingredients. Pour the mixture into the crockery. Combine the next 4 ingredients and pour over the top.

Cook on Low 4-6 hours.

← Good recipe for leftover sweet potatoes.

← It's sweet.

Thanks, Sue Anne

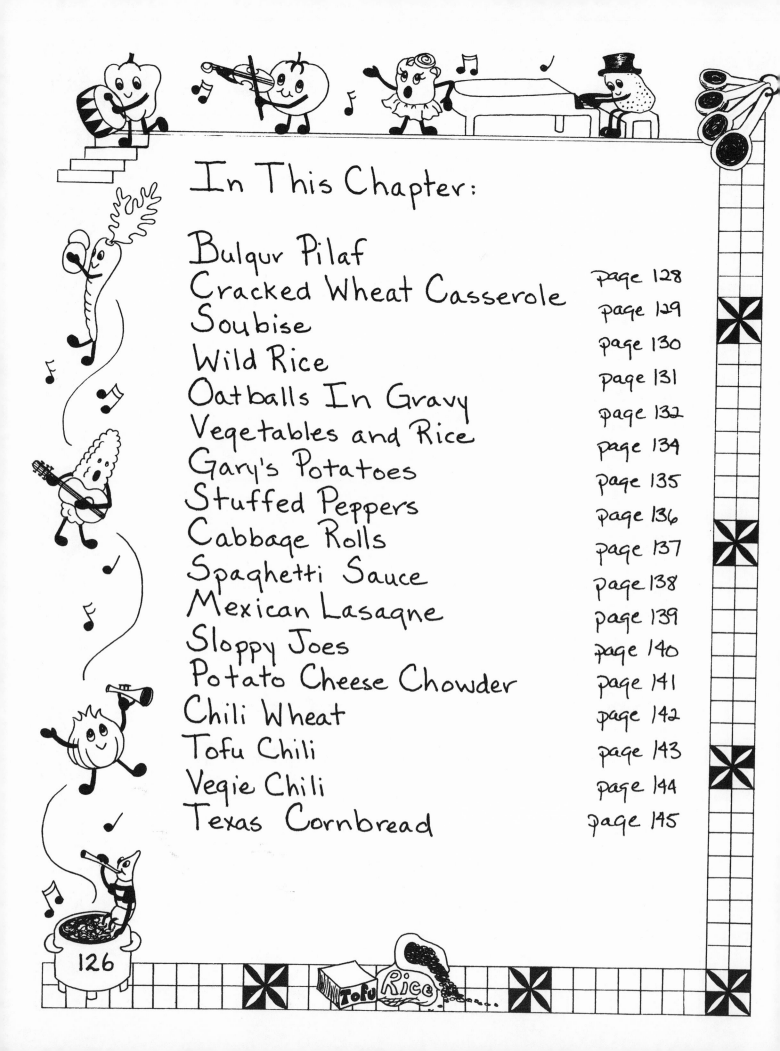

In This Chapter:

Bulgur Pilaf — page 128
Cracked Wheat Casserole — page 129
Soubise — page 130
Wild Rice — page 131
Oatballs In Gravy — page 132
Vegetables and Rice — page 134
Gary's Potatoes — page 135
Stuffed Peppers — page 136
Cabbage Rolls — page 137
Spaghetti Sauce — page 138
Mexican Lasagne — page 139
Sloppy Joes — page 140
Potato Cheese Chowder — page 141
Chili Wheat — page 142
Tofu Chili — page 143
Vegie Chili — page 144
Texas Cornbread — page 145

Bulqur Pilaf

Serves 8

2 cups bulqur
1 onion - diced
5 cups beef broth
½ cup butter - melted
2 Tbsp parsley
½ tsp salt

Combine all the ingredients in the crockery. Stir well.

Cook on Low 10-12 hours.

★ I always serve peas when I have this.

★ You can substitute soybeans for the bulqur.

Cracked Wheat Casserole

Serves 8

1 cup cracked wheat

½ stick margarine

1 stalk celery - diced

1 onion - diced

2½ cups chicken broth or beef flavored bullion

½ pound mushrooms

Combine all ingredients in your crockery.
Stir well.

Cook on Low 3-4 hours,
       High 1½ hours.

You can stir peas into this one about
½ hour before serving.
I use frozen peas - no need to defrost.

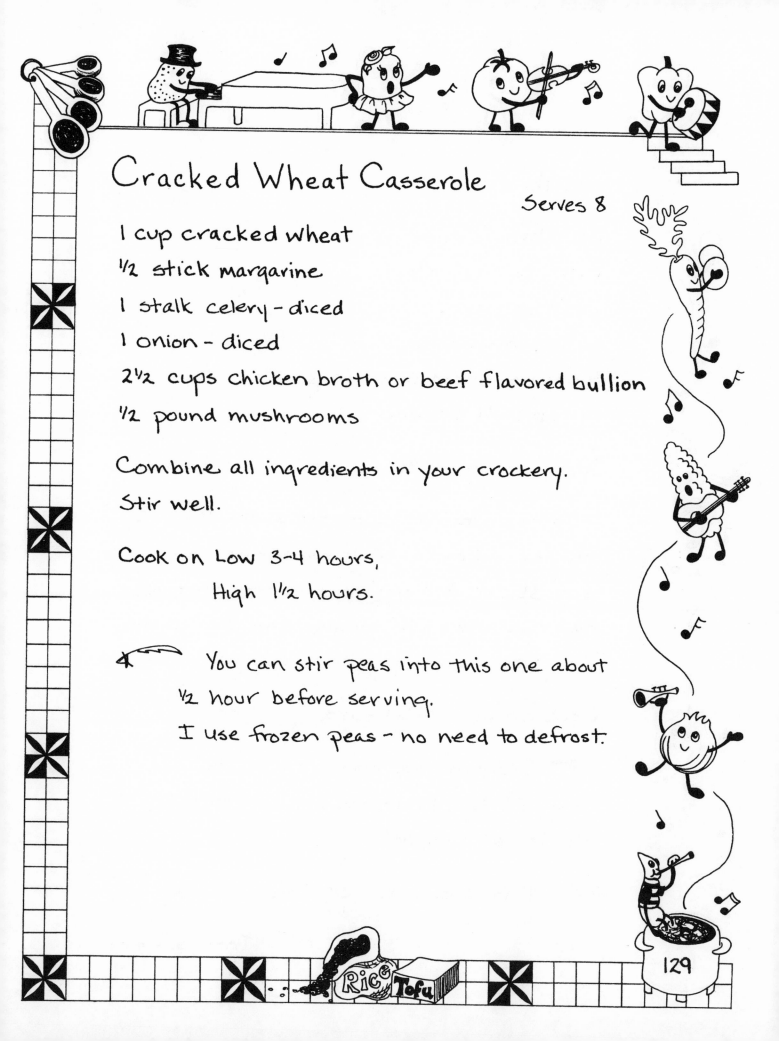

Soubise

Serves 6

1 cup brown rice

2 qts boiling water

1 tsp salt

6 Tbsp margarine

4 onions - sliced into rings

¼ tsp chili powder

Spray crockery with non-stick cooking spray.

Drop rice into boiling salted water. Boil 12 minutes and drain. Melt margarine in a large skillet. Add onions and stir to coat. Add rice and chili powder and stir again. Pour into crockery with ½ cup water.

Cook on Low 4-6 hours.

☞ You can use long grain white rice. Parboil for 7 minutes and add only ¼ cup water at the end.

☞ This is even better the next day.

☞ Thanks, Rene

130

Wild Rice

1 cup wild rice

¼ cup margarine

½ cup almonds – slivered or chopped

2 Tbsp green onion – chopped

½ pound mushrooms – sliced

3 cups chicken flavored broth

Spray crockery with non-stick cooking spray.

Wash and drain rice. Melt margarine in a large skillet. Add rice, almonds, green onions, and mushrooms. Cook, stirring until almonds are brown and mushroom tender. Pour mixture into crockery and stir in broth.

Cook on Low 6–10 hours.

☞ Wild rice is expensive, but wonderful. A special treat for the holidays.

Oatballs In Gravy

Serves 8

4½ cups water
½ cup soy sauce
4½ cups rolled oats
1 large onion- diced
2-3 Tbsp olive oil
1 cup sunflower seeds

½ tsp sage
1 tsp basil
1 tsp garlic
½ tsp Lawry's seasoning Salt
2 tsp parsley
2 Tbsp nutritional yeast

Bring water and soy sauce to a boil. Add oats and cook 8 minutes on medium. Set aside to cool. Sauté onions in oil. Add to oats with rest of the ingredients. Stir well. Form into balls and place on a cookie sheet. The mixture is sticky so have a pan of cool water to dip your hands into between each ball. These also make great patties.

Bake at 350° 10-20', turn and bake 10-20 minutes longer.
Place in crockery with gravy.
Cook on Low 'til ready to eat. Holds all day.
★—Thanks, Grace

Gravy

3/4 cup nutritional yeast   3 Tbsp soy sauce
1/4 cup flour   3/4 tsp salt
1/3 cup oil   3 cups water

In a large saucepan toast the yeast and flour (cook it dry) on medium heat. When you can smell it, add oil and stir 'til golden. Still stirring—add water. Then add soy and salt. Adjust water for desired thickness.

Peanut Butter Gravy

Same as above plus 2 Tbsp peanut butter, 1/4 tsp garlic powder, 1 tsp onion powder, and increase soy sauce to 1/4 cup. Make the same way adding peanut butter with the soy.

☞ I like the PB Gravy with oat burgers.

☞ The burgers and balls freeze well. Just wipe crockery with oil, whip up a batch of gravy and drop in the oatmeal shape of choice to warm.

133

Vegetables and Rice

Serves 6

1 cup brown rice

1 can cream of mushroom soup

1 can water (use above can)

1 green pepper - cut in large pieces

1 pkg onion soup Mix

Spray crockery with non-stick cooking spray.

Combine rice, soup and water. Stir well and pour into crockery. Place vegies in a roaster bag. Shake soup over them. Inflate bag, twisting top to trap air. Shake to coat vegies. Let air out and roll top down. Poke 3-4 holes in the top of the bag and set on top of the rice.

Cook on Low 4-6 hours.

※ Carrots, potatoes and onions are good with a bullion cube / granules.

Gary's Potatoes

Serves 6

½ cup chopped green onion

2 cups cooked potato – sliced or diced

1 pound tofu, mashed well with a fork

2 eggs – lightly beaten

1 cup sour cream

1 cup grated cheddar cheese

2 tsp Lawry's seasoned or herb salt

1 tsp garlic

Spray crockery with non-stick cooking spray.

Gently mix all ingredients in a large bowl.
Turn into crockery.

Cook on Low 6-8 hours.

Serve garnished with sour cream and grated cheddar cheese.

Everyone likes this one.

Stuffed Peppers

Serves 4

4 green bell peppers – core and seed
1 cup cooked brown rice
1 cup whole kernel corn
1 small onion – chopped
1 stalk celery – diced with leaves
4 oz cubed Monterey Jack cheese
½ tsp Lawry's seasoning salt
¼ tsp dill
pinch cayenne

Prepare peppers to be stuffed. No parboiling.
Sauté onion in large skillet. Add celery.
Add rest of ingredients and stir until
cheese melts and binds food together.
Stuff peppers and place in pot with
⅓ cup water.

Cook on Low 6-8 hours.

This stuffing works great in squash.

Cabbage Rolls

Serves 10

1 head of cabbage
1 large onion -diced
2 cloves of garlic
1-2 Tbsp olive oil
3/4 pound frozen tofu
3 eggs- beaten
1 cup cooked rice

1/2 cup raisins
1 can (15oz) tomato sauce
1/4 tsp ginger
1/2 tsp salt
1 Tbsp brown sugar
1 Tbsp vinegar
3-4 potatoes

Defrost tofu. Steam cabbage 8-10 minutes. Pull off outer 10-12 leaves for stuffing. Slice potatoes in the bottom of crockery to make a rack. To make filling - combine rest of the ingredients. Rinse, squeeze dry and crumble tofu. Stir all well and then place 2-3 Tbsp in each leaf, tuck in sides and roll. Place seam side down on potatoes.

Cook on Low 10-12 hours.

Spaghetti Sauce

Serves 10

¼ cup olive oil

3 garlic cloves - minced

1 large onion - diced

1 12 oz can tomato paste

1 46 oz can tomato juice

1 28 oz can of whole tomatoes

¼ cup parsley

1½ tsp basil

1 pinch of oregano

In a pan over medium heat, sauté the garlic and onion in olive oil. When onions are translucent, add tomato paste and blend well. Add 12 oz water (just use tomato paste can) Add spices. Add tomato juice. Heat until it bubbles. Pour into the crockery. Add whole tomatoes.

Cook on Low 6-8 hours.

➤ You can add ½ bell pepper, ⅔ cup mushrooms if desired - sauted

Mexican Lasagna

Serves 10

2 cups cooked pinto beans

1 15oz container ricotta cheese

1 cup cottage cheese

1 can (4oz) chopped green chiles

3/4 pound Monterey Jack cheese - sliced

1 batch Spaghetti Sauce or 1 large store-bought jar

3/4 pound lasagna noodles

Spray crockery with non-stick cooking spray.
Mix pinto beans with the spaghetti sauce.
Mix together ricotta, cottage cheese and chiles.
Cook lasagna noodles, drain and cut-up. I
cut them up to help fit the curve and make
serving easier. Okay. Spread a little sauce in
the bottom of the crockery (enough to cover).
Next, place 1/2 noodles, 1/2 ricotta, 1/2 sauce
and 1/2 MJ cheese. Repeat layers: rest of
noodles, ricotta, sauce and cheese.

Cook on Low 6-8 hours.

Try whole wheat or articoke lasagna for a

Thanks, Judith   treat.

139

Sloppy Joe's

Serves 6

1 pound tofu
1 onion - diced
1 green pepper - chopped
½-1 tsp garlic salt
1 tsp oregano
1 tsp basil
2 cups tomato sauce
buns or English muffins
4 oz mozzarella - grated

Sauté onions, peppers and garlic. Add tofu and herbs. Stir to blend everything. Add tomato sauce and stir again. Pour it into your crockery.

Cook on Low 6-8 hours.

I've eaten it after just 4 hours.

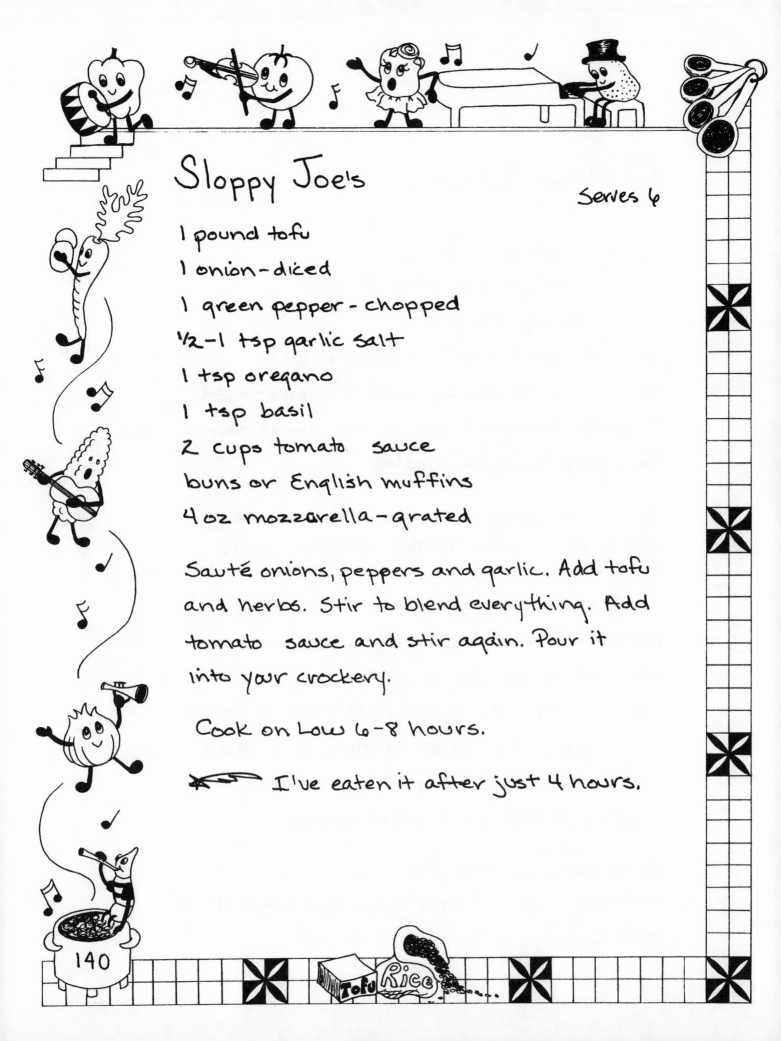

140

Potato Cheese Chowder

Serves 6

1 onion - diced

1 tsp garlic in oil (3 cloves)

3 potatoes - diced in ½" cubes

2 cans (8oz) tomato sauce

4 cups water

½ tsp salt

1 tsp beef Flavored bullion

1¼ cups grated cheddar cheese
   (or try Farmers cheese for stringy fun)

1 pound frozen tofu - thawed, rinsed, squeeze
   dry and crumbled

Combine all ingredients in crockery. Stir well.

Cook on Low 6-8 hours.

☞ Always better the next day.

☞ Soybean curd is what tofu is made from.
   It's packaged in water in one pound containers.
   Store in fresh water. Freezing changes it
   from firm to chewy consistency.

☞ Thanks, Gary

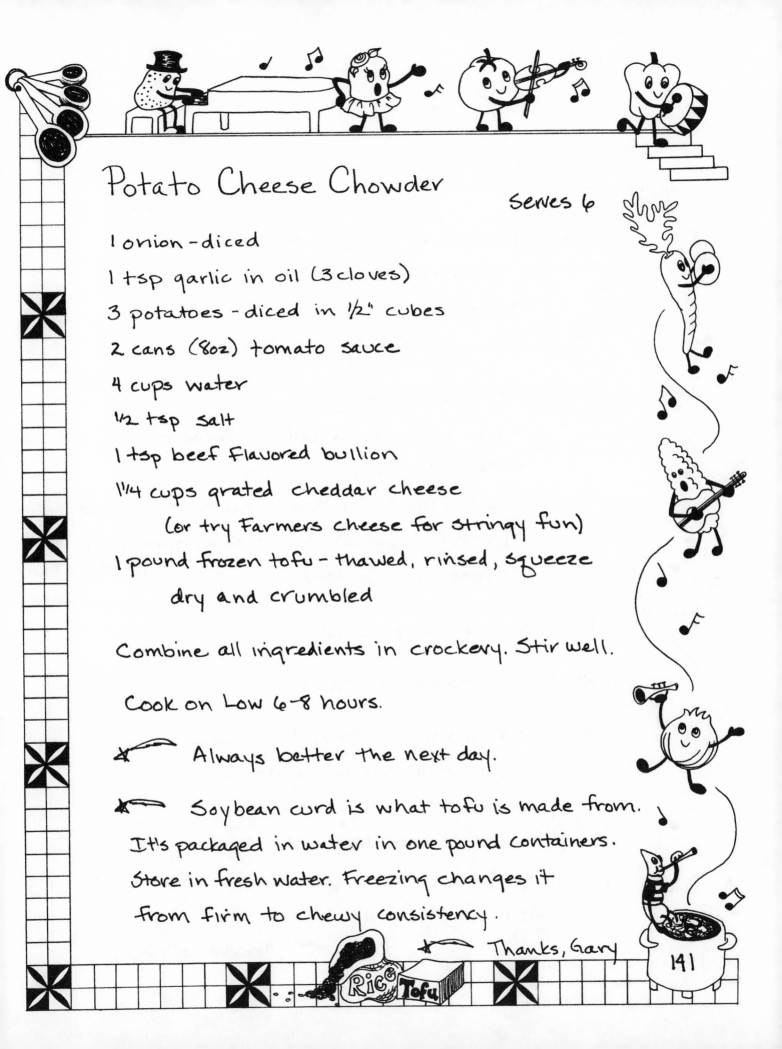

141

Chili Wheat

Serves 6

The night before: place in crockery

    1 cup kidney beans

    3 cups water

Cook on Low overnight (6-10 hours).

In the morning add:

    1 cup TVP (texturized vegetable protein)

    2 Tbsp dehydrated onions

    1 can (1lb 13oz) whole tomatoes - mashed

    1 can (use above) equal amount tomato juice

    1 Tbsp chili powder

Cook on Low 6-8 hours.

★➤ This turns out thick.

★➤ If you like hotter chili - substitute 1 package chili seasoning mix for chili powder.

★➤ You can also substitute 1 pound frozen tofu - rinsed, squeeze dried & crumbled instead of the TVP.

★➤ Thanks, Wilkinson

142

Tofu Chili

Serves 10

The night before: Place in crockery
- 1 cup kidney beans
- 3 cups water

Take tofu out of the freezer to defrost.

In the morning add:
- 3 cans (16 oz each) chili beans
- 1 pkg chili seasoning
- 1 qt canned tomatoes - mashed or 28 oz store-bought tomatoes
- 1 large onion - diced
- 1 pound frozen tofu - defrosted, rinsed, squeeze dried and crumbled

Cook on Low 8 hours.

* I use this recipe to introduce people to tofu.

* Ever tried corn dumplings in chili?

143

Vegie Chili

The night before: Place in crockery

    ½ cup chick peas

    ½ cup navy beans

    ½ cup kidney beans

    4 cups water

Cook on Low overnight (6-10 hours).

In the morning add:

    2 grated carrots

    ½ cup sliced celery

    ½ cup chopped green pepper

    ½ cup onion

    2 garlic cloves minced

    2 cups canned whole tomatoes mashed

    2 cups sliced fresh mushrooms

    2 cups tomato sauce

    1½ Tbsp chili powder

Cook on Low 6-8 hours, High 3-4 hours.

I like this one for lunch with Texas Cornbread.

Texas Cornbread

Serves 10

1½ cups yellow cornmeal

1 Tbsp baking powder

1 cup sour cream

1 cup grated cheddar cheese

1 cup onions - diced

¾ tsp salt

1 Tbsp sugar

4 eggs - beaten

1 cup cream style corn

1 cup chopped peppers (I mix green and red)

½ cup oil

½ cup margarine - melted

In a large bowl combine all ingredients
except margarine. Pour into a 9x13 pan.
Bake at 450° 20-30°.

Poke holes with a toothpick every so often
and pour melted margarine over the top.

➤ You can cook on Low 6-8 hours in your
crockery - it's moist and delicious, but falls
apart.

145

In This Chapter:

Spaghetti Pie .... page 148
Tia's Rigatoni .... page 149
Bar-B-Que Hot Dogs .... page 150
Doctored Beans .... page 151
Upside Down Supper .... page 152
Joanne's Favorite .... page 153
Yummy Crab Dip .... page 154
Claudia's Articoke Dip .... page 155
Country Apples .... page 156
French Almond Apples .... page 157
Mmm Coconut .... page 158
That's Good Peaches .... page 159
Pumpkin Job .... page 160
Spoon Peaches .... page 161
Chocolate Bread Pudding .... page 162
Triple Chocolate Mess .... page 163
Cheese Fondue .... page 164
Chocolate Fondue .... page 165
Spiced Apple Juice .... page 166

Spaghetti Pie

Serves 10

8 oz spaghetti (I like whole wheat)
2 eggs
1/3 cup Parmesan cheese
1 pound ground chuck
1 32 oz bottle of spaghetti sauce
3 cups cottage cheese
4 oz mozzarella cheese

Boil spaghetti 7-10 minutes, brown the chuck.
Drain spaghetti and cut-up. Add eggs
and parmesan. Stir well. Pour 1/2 cup
sauce on the bottom of the crockery.
Layer 1/2 pasta, 1/2 cottage cheese, 1/2 meat
    and sauce, 1/2 mozzarella.
Repeat layers.

Cover, plug in and cook on Low 6-8 hours.

— Thanks, Debbie

148

Tia's Rigatoni

Meatballs:

1-1½ pounds ground beef

Italian seasoned bread crumbs

1 egg

Parsley to taste

2-3 garlic cloves - minced

10 oz mozzarella - grated

one batch of Spaghetti Sauce or 1 large store bought jar

1 box rigatoni

1 pound ricotta cheese

2 hard boiled eggs - sliced

Combine meatball ingredients and form balls. Brown lightly while cooking pasta. Combine meatballs and sauce. Cover the bottom of the crockery with sauce.

Layer: ½ pasta, ⅓ cheese, ½ ricotta, ½ eggs

   Repeat layers ending with last ⅓ cheese

Cook on Low 6-8 hrs.

Bar-B-Que Hot Dogs

Serves 8

2 onions - diced

2 Tbsp oil

1 tsp salt

4 Tbsp brown sugar

2 cups ketchup

1 cup water

4 Tbsp vinegar

6 Tbsp worchestershire sauce

1 Tbsp mustard

2 pkg beef hot dogs or cocktail wieners

Sauté onions in oil. Cut-up hot dogs into bite-size pieces. Combine all ingredients and stir well. Pour into the crockery.

Cook on Low 6-8 hours.

150

Doctored Beans

Serves 6

3 cans (16oz) pork and beans
1 Tbsp brown sugar
1 tsp molasses
½ tsp prepared mustard
1 small onion - diced
3-4 strips bacon

Fry bacon until lightly brown. Cut-up and combine in the crockery with the rest of the ingredients.

Cook on Low 6-8 hours

Serve with "pigs-in-a-blanket" (hot dogs wrapped with a biscuit and baked).

Upside Down Supper

Serves 8

1½ cups cooked ham
1 cup cooked lima beans
1 can (16 oz) cream style corn
1 cup cheddar cheese -grated
1 Tbsp minced onion
1 tsp Worchestershire sauce

2/3 cup Bisquick
1/3 cup cornmeal
1 egg
1/4 cup milk

Mix ham, beans, corn, cheese, onion and worchestershire sauce. Pour into crockery. Mix remaining ingredients and spread batter evenly over edge of casserole. It's sticky, but manageable.

Cook on Low 6-8 hours.

152

Joanne's Favorite

Serves 8

1 pound package smoked sausage

1 pound pinto beans

7 cups water

3 garlic cloves- minced

3 small onions- diced

1 tsp salt

1 tsp Pickapeppa

Cut sausage into bite size pieces.

Combine all ingredients in crockery.

Cook on Low 8-10 hours.

Yummy Crab Dip

Serves 10

- 2 8oz cream cheese
- 2 6½ oz cans of crab meat
- 1 garlic clove – minced
- ½ cup mayonaise
- 2 tsp prepared mustard
- ¼ cup apple juice
- 1 Tbsp minced onion

Combine all ingredients and pour into crockery.

Heat through on Low 45 minutes.

Serve on small cubes of French bread.

154

Claudia's Articoke Dip

Serves 20

3 cans (14 oz) water packed articokes

1½ cups mayonaise (Hellmann's)

¾ cup Parmesan cheese

3 green onions - chopped

2 bold dashes Worchestershire sauce

3 dashes Tabasco

Squeeze water from articokes and mash with a fork. Mix with other ingredients. Pour into crockery.

Cook on Low until warm - 30-45 minutes.

Serve with crackers. Twigs are my favorite. Or try on french bread and serve with soup.

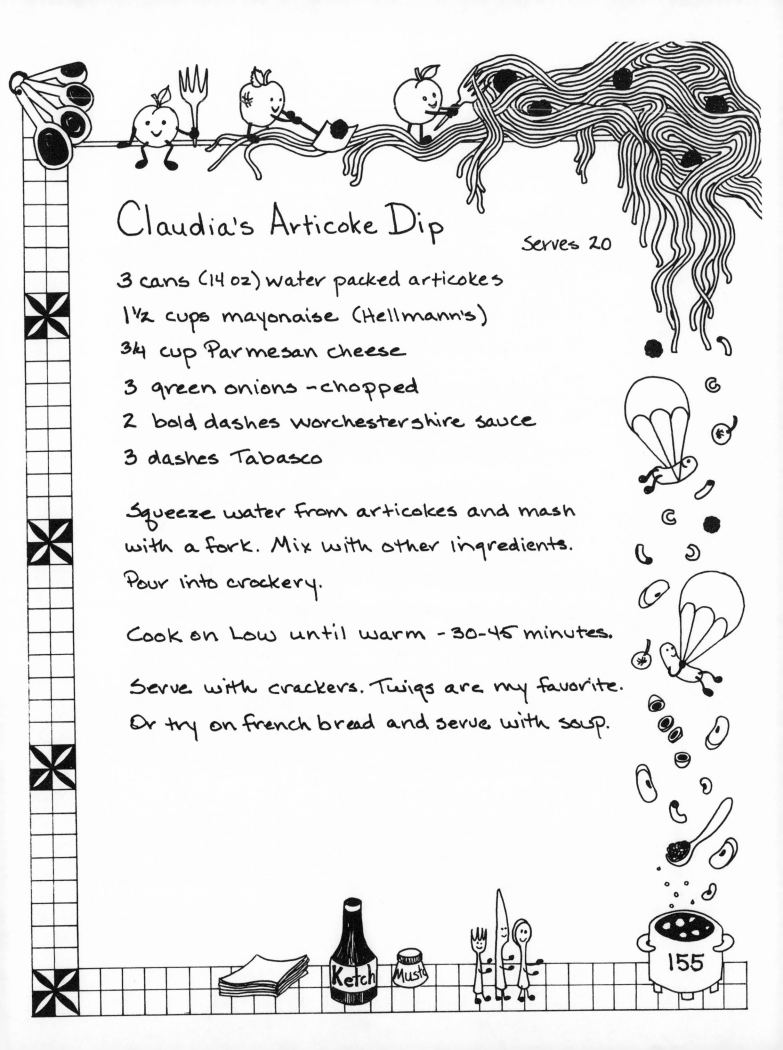

155

Country Apples

Serves 6

4-5 cups apples
2 Tbsp flour
1/3 cup sugar
1/3 cup raisins
1/4 tsp cinnamon
2/3 cup oatmeal
3 Tbsp butter
3/4 cup brown sugar

Peel, slice and coat apples with flour and 1/3 cup sugar. Stir in the raisins, cinnamon, and oatmeal. Pour 1 cup water into crockery. add apple mix. Pour melted butter over apples and then brown sugar.

Cook on Low 4-6 hours.

You can serve over vanilla ice cream, use as a crepe filling or over oatmeal for breakfast.

French Almond Apples

Serves 6

6 cups sliced apples
1¼ tsp cinnamon
¼ tsp ground nutmeg
¾ cup milk
2 Tbsp Margarine
2 eggs
1 cup sugar
½ cup Bisquick

Streusel:

1 cup Bisquick
½ cup almonds
⅓ cup brown sugar
3 Tbsp firm Margarine

Spray crockery with non-stick spray.

Mix apples with spices and pour in crockery.
In a blender beat remaining ingredients.
Pour over apples. Mix streusel ingredients
together until crumbly and sprinkle
over apples.

Cook on Low 6-8 hours.

Mmm Coconut

Serves 6

2 cups milk

¼ cup margarine

1½ tsp vanilla

4 eggs

1 cup flaked coconut (or shredded)

3/4 cup sugar

½ cup Bisquick

Place all ingredients in the blender. Mix well. Pour into crockery.

Cook on Low 8-10 hours.

158

That's Good Peaches

Serves 4

4 cups sliced peaches
1/3 cup Bisquick
2/3 cup oatmeal
1/4 tsp cinnamon
1/2 cup sugar
1/2 cup brown sugar

Spray crockery with non-stick spray.

Mix dry ingredients together. Stir
in peaches and pour in crockery.

Cook on Low 4-6 hours.

Thanks, Mary Sue

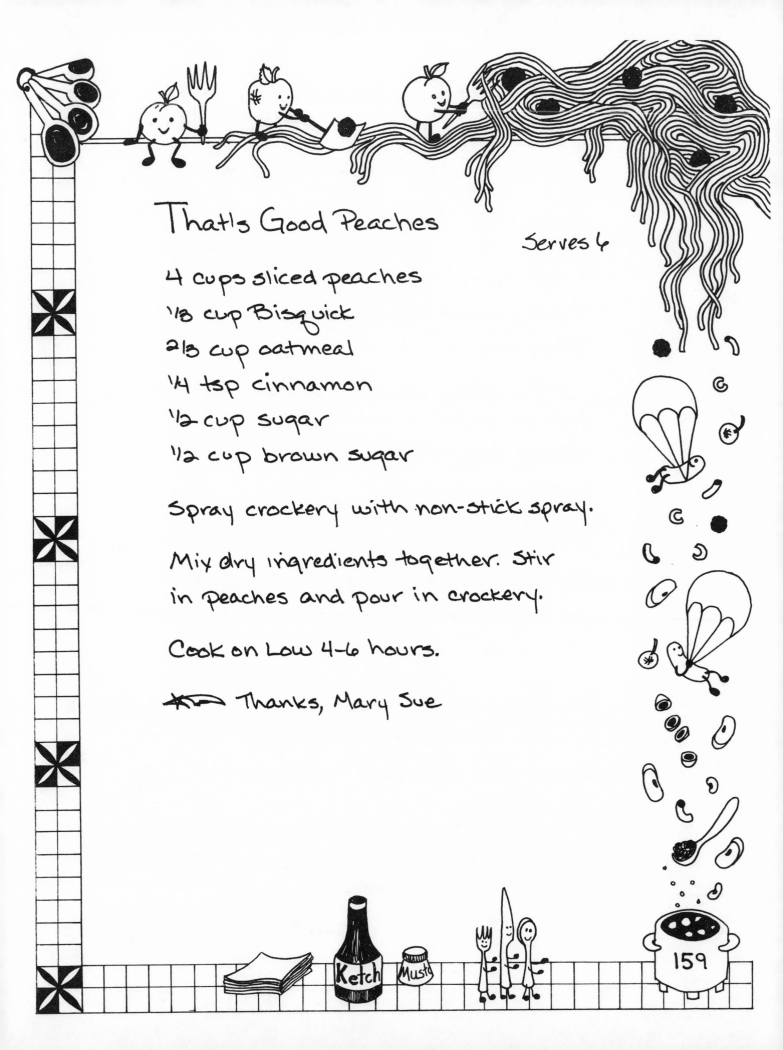

Pumpkin Job

Serves 6

1 can (16 oz) pumpkin

2½ tsp pumpkin pie spice

2 tsp vanilla

1 can evaporated milk

3/4 cup sugar

½ cup Bisquick

2 Tbsp margarine

2 eggs

Spray crockery with non-stick spray.
Beat ingredients together until smooth
with a hand mixer. Pour into crockery.

Cook on Low 6-8 hours,
        High 3-4 hours.

Spoon into cups and top with cool whip.

☞ This was named when a teenager, Shane,
walked into the dining room and asked
"Where's some of that pumpkin job?"
☞ Thanks, Shane

Spoon Peaches

Serves 6

1/3 cup white sugar

1/2 cup brown sugar

2 tsp melted margarine

1/2 can evaporated milk

3/4 cup Bisquick

2 eggs

2 cups peaches - mashed

2 tsp vanilla

3/4 tsp cinnamon

Spray crockery with non-stick spray.

Combine sugar and Bisquick. Add eggs and vanilla. Add margarine and milk. Add peaches and cinnamon. Pour into crockery.

Cook on Low 6-8 hours.

161

Chocolate Bread Pudding

Serves 6

1 pkg (6 oz) semi sweet chocolate chips

1 1/2 cups Bisquick

1/2 cup nuts - chopped (optional)

1/3 cup sugar

1/2 cup milk

2 Tbsp vegetable oil

1 tsp vanilla

1 egg

1 1/2 cups hot water

2/3 cup sugar

Spray crockery with non-stick spray.

Melt chocolate chips. In a bowl mix Bisquick, nuts, 1/3 cup sugar, milk, oil, vanilla, and egg. Beat vigorously. Add melted chips. Pour into crockery. Heat water and disolve 2/3 cup sugar. Pour over top.

Cook on Low 8-10 hours.

Serve with ice cream or cool whip.

Triple Chocolate Mess

Serves 8

1 pkg chocolate cake mix

1 pt sour cream

1 pkg instant chocolate pudding mix

1 small bag chocolate chips

3¼ cup oil

4 eggs

1 cup water

Spray crockery with non-stick spray.

Mix all ingredients until smooth.
Pour into crockery.

Cook on Low 6-8 hours.

Serve in a bowl with vanilla ice cream.

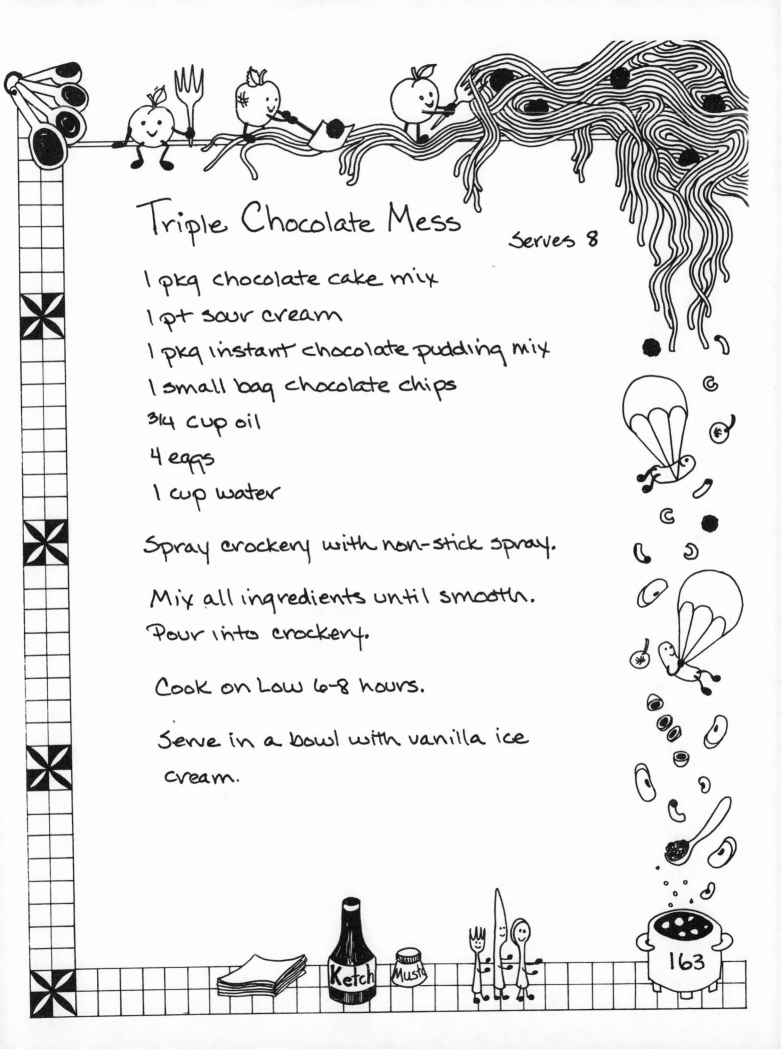

Cheese Fondue

Serves 10

6 Tbsp butter or margarine
9 Tbsp flour
3 cups milk
1½ pounds Swiss cheese - grated
¼ tsp garlic salt
pinch nutmeg

Melt butter and add flour stirring until blended. Gradually stir in milk. Cook 2-3 minutes over low heat. Add cheese by the handfuls, stirring until the cheese melts. Add garlic and nutmeg. Pour into crockery.

Keep warm on Low. Makes almost ½ pot. Dip with toasted french bread.

☞ I only use my crockery for fondue when it needs to travel or when dealing with young kids. My brownies loved it.

☞ You can thin it with a little milk.

Chocolate Fondue

Serves 12

6 9-ounce milk chocolate candy bars
6 1-ounce squares semi-sweet baking chocolate
3 cups light cream (half and half)

Break chocolate into pieces and place in a
large pan. Cover with cream. Turn heat
on low and melt chocolate. Stir constantly.
Pour into crockery.

Keep warm on Low. Makes almost ½ pot.
Dip with bananas, cheeries, pineapple,
    pear, strawberries, angel food cake,
    or fingers, popcorn, oranges or grapes.

* To convert either cheese or
chocolate fondue recipe to a
fondue pot - only use ⅓ amount.

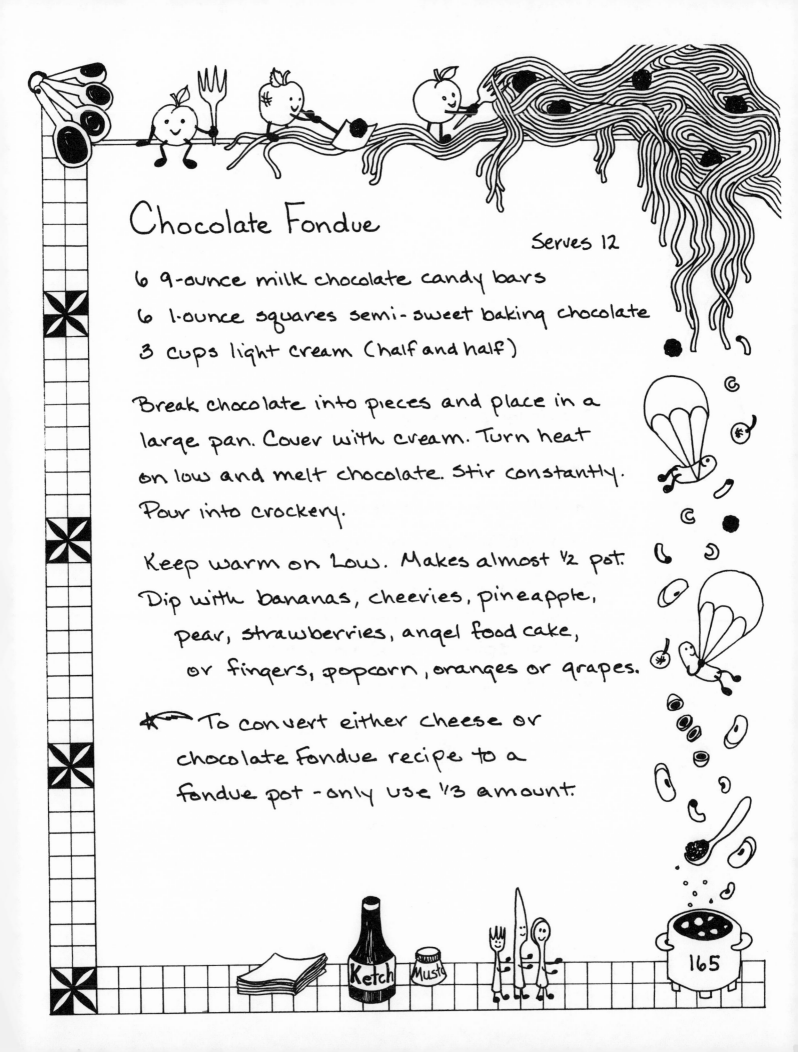

Spiced Apple Juice

Serves 8

½ cup brown sugar
2 qts cider
1 tsp whole allspice
1½ tsp whole cloves
2 sticks cinnamon

Use a spice bag to contain the spices.
It makes for easy removal. Combine
all ingredients in crockery.

Cook on Low 2-8 hours.

Remove spices, ladel into cups and
garnish with orange slices.

This makes the house smell so
good, it's worth doing a pot full
just for the aroma.

Elephant Stew

Serves the entire neighborhood

one elephant
handfull of wild potatoes
handfull of wild onions (ramps)
elephant garlic (minced)
peppergrass
fireweed
* wild honey for sweetening with older elephants

You'll need:
3 sharp knives
sharpening stone

Skin and debone meat- in the bathtub.
You will need to trim the meat to fit the crockery. Cram and squeeze until all is in.

Cook on Low 38 hours.

→ While bagging elephant be sure to grab some wild tundra grass seed to thicken stew.

→ Just stuff leftovers in the trunk.

→ Serve on a platter of watercress and wild rice.

→ Thanks, Deb

Ketch   Musta

Appendix I - Calorie Count

Page		Calories Per Serving	Page		Calories Per Serving
Good Things To Get Up To			**Eating Off The Range**		
20	Cream of Wheat	30	54	Pot Roast	465
21	Breakfast Oatmeal	75	55	John's Goulash	368
22	Country Style Kasha	81	56	Shirley's Ragout	195
23	Millet Cereal	54	57	French Dip	316
24	Spiced Prunes	70	58	Mom's Meatloaf	281
25	Dried Fruit Compote	165	59	Meatballs and Gravy	230
26	Baked Apples	211	60	Great Glazed Corned Beef	423
27	Chunky Applesauce	64	61	Ruebens	530
28	Plain Rice	168	62	Meatballs	258
29	Breakfast Potatoes	203	63	Chops and Kraut	440
30	Travelin' Eggs	314	64	Joe's Pork Chops and Rice	399
31	Breakfast Spinach	199	65	Barbie-Q-Delight...Tofu	192
			65	...Chicken	305
			65	...Tenderloin	613
			65	...Ribs	568
			66	Peasant Stew	735
			67	Lamb Chops	560
			68	Lamb Curry	486
			69	Lamb Stew	963
			70	Country Ham	327
			71	Honey-Orange Glazed Ham	208
Pour It In The Pot			**Sunday Brunch**		
34	Good Ole Stew	458	74	Roaster Bag Chicken	535
35	Refrigerator Stew	267	75	Barbie-Que In A Bag	418
36	Martha's Creation	87	76	Finger Lickin' Chicken	501
37	Meatball Stew	167	77	Chicken al la Fruit	486
38	Kat's Greek Stew	261	78	Cranberry Chicken	718
39	Vegie Soup A La El	121	79	Great Chicken	685
40	Tortilla Soup	418	80	Chicken Catch-A-Tory	498
41	Turkey Soup	146	81	Garlic Chicken	485
42	Steak Soup	608	82	Spicy Chicken Wings	204
43	'A Little Bit of This' Soup	105	83	Chicken and Dumplings	462
44	Patti's Potato Soup	85	84	Chicken Broccoli Casserole	418
44	Clam Chowder	160	85	Chicken Casserole	510
45	Split Pea Soup	120	86	Chicken Risotto	469
46	Chick Pea Soup	239	87	Usable Chicken	225
47	Lentil Soup	189			
48	Pea Beans	130			
49	Country Pintos	124			
50	Fritz's Chili	355			
51	Prisicilla's Chili	360			

Page		Calories Per Serving
Mexican Delights		
90	Mexican Meat	142
91	Refried Beans	46
92	Burritos *	265
94	Soft Tacos *	250
95	Tostadas *	335
96	Taquitos *	195
97	Guacamole (entire batch)	1400
98	Taco Salad	446
99	Bean Dip	331
100	Tamale Casserole	299
101	Chili Rellanos	185
102	Mexican Gravy	101
103	Chicken Enchiladas	288
104	Mexican Style Tasty Goop	291
105	Salsa (entire batch)	135

Page		Calories Per Serving
For My Vegitarian Friends		
128	Bulgur Pilaf	169
129	Cracked Wheat Casserole	215
130	Soubise	232
131	Wild Rice	374
132	Oatballs In Gravy	276
134	Vegetables and Rice	192
135	Gary's Potatos	270
136	Stuffed Peppers	282
137	Cabbage Rolls	99
138	Spaghetti Sauce	114
139	Mexican Lasagne	321
140	Sloppy Joes	174
141	Potato Cheese Chowder	233
142	Chili Wheat **	201
143	Tofu Chili	107
144	Vegie Chili	99
145	Texas Cornbread	396

Page		Calories Per Serving
Vegies		
108	Acorn Squash	33
109	Butternut Squash	33
110	Zucchini Squash	357
111	Cauliflower Casserole	180
112	Green Bean Bake	148
113	Corn Pudding	272
114	Glazed Carrots	146
115	Chinese Cabbage	63
116	Asperagus A La Ayers	103
117	Creamy Cheesy Corn	242
118	Broccoli Corn Bread	226
119	Broccoli Casserole	366
120	Scalloped Potatoes	117
121	Cheese Potatoes	346
122	Baked Potatoes	75
123	Ella's Potatoes	258
124	Baked Onions	38
125	Butternut Squash Delight	539

Page		Calories Per Serving
Kids' Favorites		
148	Spaghetti Pie	342
149	Tia's Rigatoni	856
150	Bar - B - Que Hot Dogs	383
151	Doctored Beans	165
152	Upside Down Supper	259
153	Joanne's Favorite	306
154	Yummy Crab Dip	260
155	Claudia's Articoke Dip	211
156	Country Apples	312
157	French Almond Apples	144
158	Mmm Coconut	418
159	That's Good Peaches	224
160	Pumpkin Job	282
161	Spoon Peaches	246
162	Chocolate Bread Pudding	457
163	Triple Chocolate Mess	775
164	Cheese Fondue	373
165	Chocolate Fondue	898
166	Spiced Apple Juice	139

*Includes maximum amounts of all optional ingredients

** Calculated with tofu because T.V.P. calories unavailable

Appendix II
High Fiber Recipes

Page Recipe

21 Breakfast Oatmeal
22 Country Style Kasha
23 Millet Cereal
24 Spiced Prunes
25 Dried Fruit Compote
26 Baked Apples – with peels
28 Plain Rice – brown rice
29 Breakfast Potatoes – with peels

34 Good Ole Stew
35 Refrigerator Stew
36 Martha's Creation
37 Meatball Stew
41 Turkey Gumbo – with brown rice
42 Steak Soup – with potato skins
43 "A Little Bit Of This" Soup
45 Split Pea Soup
46 Chick Pea Soup
47 Lentil Soup
48 Pea Bean
49 Country Pintos
50 Fritz's Chili
51 Prisicillia's Chili

54 Pot Roast – with potato skins
55 John's Goulash – with peelings
56 Shirley's Ragout – with peelings
64 Joe's Pork Chops and rice – with brown rice

129 Cracked Wheat Casserole
130 Soubise

151 Doctored Beans
152 Upside Down Supper

NOTES

For page numbers listed under recipe titles, see Calorie Appendix Page 166 and 167

APOLOGY

I apologize for any mistakes or errors. It's my writing, so I'm the one to blame. It seems impossible to catch them all. My goal was to gather all my favorite recipes for you with clear, concise, communication. If you have any questions, comments, or even complaints or compliments, please contact me. I tried my best, and as Hawkeye Pierce once said on M.A.S.H "Best is Best."

Star Feather Productions
PO Box 1986
Sylva, NC 28779

Barb Nesten

You can order CROCK-IT from the above address. Just send $12.95 plus $3.00 postage and handling. NC residence need to add 5% tax. So that's $15.95 or $16.60

God Bless

172

Index

'A Little Bit of This' Soup 20
Abbreviations 176
Acorn Squash 108
Allspice 108,166
Almonds 86,131,157
Angel food cake 165
Appendix 168,169,170
Apples 27,29,69,68,156,157
Apple Juice 27,76,86,159
          Cider 166
Applesauce 63
Apricots 25
Artichokes 155
Asparagus A La Ayers 116
Avocados 97,99

Bacon 29,36,47,151
Baked Apples 26
Baked Potatoes 122
Baked Onions 124
Bananas 165
Barbecue, Chicken 65
          Hot Dogs 150
          In A Bag 75
          Tenderloin 65
          Tofu 65
          Ribs 65
Barley 67
Bay Leaf 38,40,41,48,60,68,87
Beans, fifteen 38
          green 35,42,43
          pea (great northern) 48
          pinto 49,51,91,139,153
          lima 152
          navy 144
          pork n' 151
Beef, corned 60,61
          ground 37,50,51,58,59,62,64,
          98,100,148,149
          steak 42
          stew 34,35,39,55,56,90
          roast 54,57
Beef broth   (see Bullion)
Bell peppers .... see green peppers
Bisquick 30,31,84,110,152,158,159160,161,162
Bread Crumbs 61,151
Breakfast Oatmeal 21
Breakfast Potatoes 29
Breakfast Spinach 31
Broccoli 83,116,119
Broccoli Casserole 119
Broccoli Corn Bread 118
Brown Sugar 28,38,58,60,70,79,125
          137,150,151,156,159,161,166
Buckwheat groats 22
Bulgur Pilaf 127

Bullion, beef 34,42,57,128,141
          chicken 68,85,102,104,131
          vegetable 28
Burritos 92
Butternut Squash Delight 125
Butternut Squash 109

Cabbage 60,115,137
Cabbage Rolls 137
Carrots 34,35,36,39,42,43,45,54,55
          56,59,60,66,69,71,78,114,122
Catalina dressing 69
Cauliflower Casserole 111
Cayenne 136
Celery 36,39,41,42,43,64
          66,68,129,136,144
Cheese 29,92,94,95,111,120,121
          American 99
          Cheddar 30,40,83,98,101,104
          116,119,135,141,145,152
          Farmer 141
          Monterey Jack 51,101,136,139
          Mozzarella 140,148,149
          Parmesan 30,83,86,110,148,155
          Ricotta 139,149
          Swiss 30,31,61,164
Cheese Fondue 164
Cheese Potatoes 121
Cherries 165
Chick Pea Soup 46
Chick Peas 46,144
Chicken 65,74,75,76,77,78,79,80,81
          82,83,84,85,86,87,103,104
Chicken A La Fruit 77
Chicken and Dumplings 83
Chicken Broccoli Casserole 84
Chicken broth   (see Bullion)
Chicken Casserole 85
Chicken Catch-A-Tory 80
Chicken Enchiladas 103
Chicken Risotto 86
Chili beans 50,143
Chili powder 64,91,100,102,130,142,144
Chili sauce 62
Chili seasoning 50,51,143
Chocolate, candy bar 165
          cake mix 163
          chips 162,163
          pudding mix 163
          semi-sweet 165
Cinnamon 29,108,109,114,156,157,159,161,166
Cinnamon Stick 24,38,166
Clam Chowder 44
Claudia's Artichoke Dip 155
Cloves 30,38,166
Cocktail Wieners 152

Index

Coconut 126,158
Conversions 176
Corn 34,35,43,100,113,114,117,136,152
Corn Pudding................................... 113
Cornmeal 100,113,118,145,152
Cottage cheese 22,118,139,148
Country Apples............................... 159
Country Ham................................ 70
Country Pintos............................... 49
Country Style Kasha 22
Crab 159
Crackers 119,155
Cracked Wheat Casserole................ 129
Cranberry Chicken 78
Cream cheese 85,117,123,154
Cream, light................................... 165
Cream of Wheat........................... 20
Creamy onion soup........................ 66
Creamy garlic dressing 81
Cumin 38,40,91,102
Curry Powder.............................. 68

Dill 136
Dillweed 37
Doctored Beans............................ 151
Dressing....................................... 85
Dried Fruit Compote...................... 25

Eggs 30,31
English muffins 140
Evaporated milk.................. 101,125,160,161

Fifteen beans 36
Finger Lickin Chicken.................... 76
Five fragrance 82
French Almond Apples.................. 157
French dressing............................ 69,78
French fried onions...................... 112
French Dip.................................... 57
Fritz's Chili................................ 51

Garlic Chicken 81
Gary's Potatoes............................ 135
Ginger 82,137
Glazed Carrots 114
Good Ole Stew............................ 34
Grapes 112,165
Grape jelly.................................... 62
Great Chicken 79
Great Glazed Corned Beef.............. 60
Green Bean Bake......................... 112
Green beans 35,42,43,49,66,112
Green chiles.......... 90,101,103,104,105,139
Green onion 82,98,131,135,141,155
Green pepper........... 37,41,43,80,134,140,145
Guacamole................................... 97
        used in........................ 94,95,96,98

Ham 30,41,70,71,152
Hamhock................................ 45,48,154
Honey 71,82,114,126
Honey Orange Glazed Ham.................. 71
Hot dogs 150
Hot sauce 92,94,95,99

Jalapenos..................................... 50
Joanne's Favorite 153
Joe's Pork Chops and Rice............... 64
John's Goulash............................ 55

Kat's Greek Stew........................... 38
Kidney beans........... 37,50,55,142,143,144,145

Lamb 66,68,69
Lamb chops.................................. 67
Lamb Curry................................. 68
Lamb Stew................................... 69
Lasagne 139
Lawrys 59,87,97,123,132,135,136
Lemon juice................ 25,77,97,98,114
Lentil Soup................................. 47
Lettuce 92,94,95
Lima beans 152

Mmm Coconut............................ 158
Macaroni..................................... 37,55
Mace 68
Maple syrup................................ 27,71
Martha's Creation........................ 36
Mashed potatoes.......................... 49
Measurements............................. 176
Meatballs..................................... 62
Meatballs and Gravy..................... 59
Meatball Stew.............................. 37
Mexican Gravy............................ 102
Mexican Lasagna......................... 139
Mexican Meat.............................. 90
Mexican Style Tasty Goop 104
Millet Cereal............................... 23
Millet burgers............................. 23
Mushrooms........... 36,76,80,111,114,131,144

Nutmeg 31,108,157
Nutritional yeast........................ 132,133

Oatballs In Gravy 132
Oatmeal 21,132,156,159
Okra 41
Olives 98,103
Onion soup mix 35,54,57,66,67,74,134
Orange juice.............................. 71
Oregano 40,91,102,138,140

Pasta   (see Lasagna,Macaroni,Spaghetti,Rigatoni)
Patti's Potato Soup...................... 44
Pea Beans.................................... 48
Peaches 77,159,163

Index

Peanut butter 133
Pear 165
Peas 34,42,116,134
Peasant Stew...66
Pickling spice...56
Pimentos..41
Pineapple......................................59,70,77,165
Pinto beans.....................49,51,91,139,153
Pork n' beans...151
Pork, chops..63,64
          ground 100
          tenderloin.....................................65
Potatoes 29,34,35,39,42,44,54,55
                        56,60,120-123,135,137,141
Potato Cheese Chowder.................................141
Prisicilla's Chili...51
Prunes 24,25
Pumpkin..43,160
Pumpkin Job..160

Raisins 21,27,28,38,137,156
Red hots 107
Red peppers 145
Refried Beans..91
Ribs 65
Rice 28,41,56,59,64,74,75,86
                        109,130,131,134,136,137
Ricotta cheese.....................................139,149
Rigatoni 149
Rolled oats   (see oatmeal)

Sage 58,132
Salsa 97
Salt pork..46,49
Sauerkraut...49,61,63
Sausage 51,80,153
Scalloped Potatoes.......................................120
Shake 'n' Bake 75
Shirley's Ragout...56
Sloppy Joe's..140
Soft Tacos...94
Soubise...130
Soy Sauce...............77,79,82,112,132,133
Spaghetti...148
Spaghetti Pie...148
Spaghetti Sauce...138
          used in..............................80,139,148,149
Spiced Apple Juice......................................166
Spiced Prunes...24
Spicy Chicken Wings......................................82
Spinach..31
Split Pea Soup...45
Split peas 45,48
Spoon Peaches..161
Sprouts 23,92,94,95
Squash 43,108,109,125,134

Steak Soup...42
Stewed tomatoes...........................36,37,39,56
Strawberries..165
Stuffed Peppers 136
Sunflower seeds...132
Sweet potatoes...70,71

Taco Salad...98
Taco sauce..97,99
Taco seasoning..94,98,99
Tamale Casserole...100
Taquitos..96
That's Good Peaches.....................................159
Texas Cornbread..145
Tia's Rigatoni...149
Tofu-fresh...................................65,135,140
          frozen..........................137,141,144
Tomatoes -canned.................40,41,42,50,51,100,138
                              142,143,144
          fresh...............41,43,92,94,95,97,98,105
          stewed......................36,37,39,55,56
Tomato juice..............................43,79,138,142
Tomato paste...38,138
Tomato sauce.......47,55,94,101,102,137,140,141 ,145
Tomato soup..34
Tortilla soup..40
Tortillas-corn..................40,94,95,96,103,104
          flour...42
Tostadas 95
Travelin' Eggs..30
Triple Chocolate Mess....................................163
Turkey 41,87
Turkey Soup..41
Turnip 39
TVP 142

Upside Down Supper......................................152
Usable Chicken..87

V-8 juice..115
Vanilla 24,126,158,160,161,162
Vegetable Soup..43
Vegetable and Rice..134
Vegie Chili..144
Vegie Soup a La El 39
Venison 56

Walnuts 125,162
Water chestnuts...116
Wheat germ 27
Wild rice 131

Yellow squash..45
Yogurt 22
Yummy Crab Dip...154

Zucchini Souffle..110

Measurements

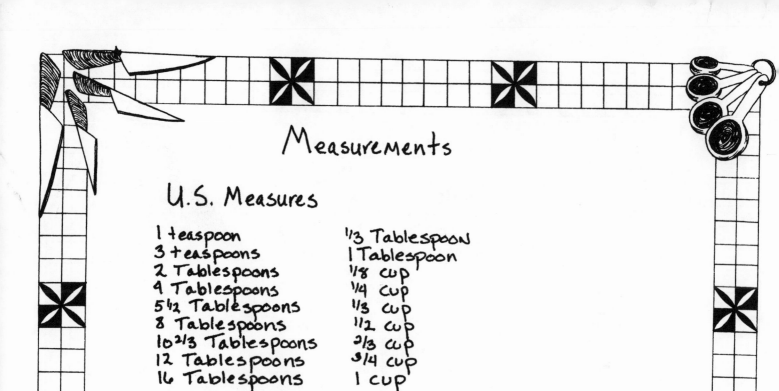

U.S. Measures

1 teaspoon	1/3 Tablespoon
3 teaspoons	1 Tablespoon
2 Tablespoons	1/8 cup
4 Tablespoons	1/4 cup
5 1/2 Tablespoons	1/3 cup
8 Tablespoons	1/2 cup
10 2/3 Tablespoons	2/3 cup
12 Tablespoons	3/4 cup
16 Tablespoons	1 cup

Liquid Measures

1 teaspoon	1/6 ounce
1 Tablespoon	1/2 ounce
2 Tablespoons	1 ounce
8 Tablespoons	1/2 cup or 4 ounces
16 Tablespoons	1 cup or 8 ounces
1 cup	1/2 pint or 8 ounces
2 cups	1 pint or 16 ounces
2 pints or 4 cups	1 quart or 32 ounces
4 quarts	1 gallon

Dry Measures

8 quarts	1 peck
40 pecks	1 bushel
1 pound	16 ounces

Abbreviations

tsp = teaspoon	oz = ounces
Tbsp = Tablespoon	pkg = package
C = cup	" = inch
° = degrees	

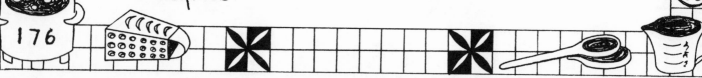